THE STRUCTURE OF AWARENESS

Volume 41, Sage Library of Social Research

SAGE LIBRARY OF SOCIAL RESEARCH

The Structure of Awareness

Toward a Symbolic Language of Human Reflexion

VLADIMIR A. LEFEBVRE

Translated from the Russian
and with a
Foreword by ANATOL RAPOPORT

Volume 41
SAGE LIBRARY OF
SOCIAL RESEARCH

SAGE PUBLICATIONS   Beverly Hills   London

For information address:

SAGE PUBLICATIONS, INC.
275 South Beverly Drive
Beverly Hills, California 90212

SAGE PUBLICATIONS LTD
St George's House / 44 Hatton Garden
London EC1N 8ER

Printed in the United States of America

Library of Congress Cataloging in Publication Data

Lefebvre, Vladimir A
 The structure of awareness.

 (Sage library of social research ; v. 41)
 Translation of Konfliktuiushchie struktury.
 Includes bibliographical references.
 1. Psychology—Methodology. 2. Introspection.
3. Awareness. I. Title.
BF38.5.L4213   153.4'22'018   76-51843
ISBN 0-8039-0720-6
ISBN 0-8039-0721-4 pbk.

FIRST PRINTING

CONTENTS

Erik Yudin
Philosopher
1930-1976
In Memoriam

ACKNOWLEDGEMENT

I am deeply thankful to Professor Anatol Rapoport for his extensive work on the translation of my book and for his detailed analysis in the foreword. His many comments in the course of the translation helped me to make the format clearer than it might have been. Moreover, the criticism in the foreword has caused me to look again at many of the problems dealt with in the book.

FOREWORD

This book, originally entitled *Konfliktuiushchie struktury,* is an example of a nonconformist philosophical investigation published in the Soviet Union. One must assume that such instances are rare. For at least forty years, Soviet philosophical discussions appearing in print have reiterated an officially sanctioned doctrine, called dialectical materialism, which is declared to underlie the officially sanctioned political doctrine called Marxism-Leninism. The impossibility of separating philosophy from politics is an axiom in the latter doctrine, and it appears to the guardians of orthodoxy that the slightest deviation from the tenets of dialectical materialism serves to subvert the political doctrine and so to "blunt the weapon of class struggle." This idea was forcefully expressed by Lenin almost seventy years ago in his philosophical monograph, *Materialism and Empirio-Criticism:*

> You cannot eliminate even one basic assumption, one substantial part of this philosophy . . . (it is as if it were a solid block of steel) without falling into the arms of bourgeois-reactionary falsehood.

Dread of deviation (nibbling at the bait in a trap set by the world bourgeoisie) imposed not only a stagnation in approved philosophical thought in the Soviet Union but also a depressing uniformity on the very language of published philosophical discussion. Not only can nothing suggesting heresy be said, as a rule, in published discussions in the Soviet

[9]

Union, but even the orthodox doctrine must be presented in the same clichés. Unusual or imaginative or less stereotyped formulations of even the sanctioned tenets would arouse suspicion.

For this reason, "dialectical materialism" and "Marxism-Leninism," when they denote official Soviet philosophy and political theory are justifiably put in quotation marks. They no longer represent substantive, indeed defensible positions that they may once have represented. Stylized reiteration has reduced these modes of thinking to compulsive verbiage, a manifestation of symptoms, perhaps, but not of analytic thinking.

The publication of *Konfliktuiushchie struktury,* therefore, appears as an anomaly, if only because *Materialism and Empirio-Criticism* is not cited in it. (I know of no other Soviet book or article dealing with philosophical questions related to scientific methodology, as this book does, that shows this glaring omission.) How this happened I do not know. Nor do I know whether the author's subsequent emigration to the United States was a consequence; nor whether the publication of this book in the Soviet Union was a harbinger of a change of intellectual climate. It may, of course, have been a trial balloon, sent up by sympathizers in the publishing establishment. In literature, several such balloons were sent up in the years of "de-Stalinization" (all eventually shot down). In philosophy, this is the only attempt known to me.

I categorize this book as philosophy, although the author probably intended it as a contribution to psychology. Actually, there is little divergence between the two views, because the author accepts introspection as the epistemological basis of his approach to psychology. Psychology rested primarily on this basis when it was regarded as a branch of philosophy. A shift of basis occurred, as Lefebvre points out, in an attempt to make psychology "scientific." The resulting behaviorist framework of thought, he contends, in adhering rigidly to the epistemology of the natural sciences, had two deleterious effects on psychology. First, it deprived psychology of a methodological tool specifically suited for it. Second, it by-passed a most important characteristic of phenomena involving interactions among "reflexive" organisms, namely the fact that *images* of things and events and also images of these images, and so on to higher orders of "reflexion," cannot be disentangled from the things and events themselves when we pursue psychological investigations.

The task undertaken by Lefebvre was that of reviving the old introspective method of psychology and of extending it to the social context, where a "persona" not only contemplates his own images but also constructs in his own mind images contemplated by others. To link this method with "scientific" psychology (demanding certain standards of rigor in formulation), Lefebvre undertook to design a formal language. He calls his method "reflexive analysis." How far he has advanced in this direction is left to the judgement of the reader. Expecting some judgements to be harsh, I will anticipate them not so much with the view of meeting the objections (some of which I have raised myself) as with the view of placing the work in proper perspective.

After presenting his epistemological position, Lefebvre starts his task by constructing an "algebra," in which images, images of images, etc. can be "registered." Thus, if T represents a portion of objective reality, or, more properly, a reality as it appears to some external observer, and X, Y, ... are personae (actors), Tx is the image of T "within" X, Txy is the image within Y of the image within X, etc. The "state of the system," reflecting the presence of images of various orders in the minds of the actors, is designated by a "reflexive polynomial," a sum of terms like those mentioned. An "act of awareness" is represented by "multiplying" the state of the system by an "operator of awareness" (also a polynomial but one not containing T), which brings the system into a new state. Thus, both the statics (description of states) and the dynamics (evolution of states) are registered in the notation. How this algebra is to be used is a legitimate question pertaining to the methodology of psychology to which the proposed scheme of representation is purported to be a contribution. Lefebvre offers examples. He translates a literary passage contributed by himself (cf. p. 51) and also a poem by Lermontov (cf. p. 106) into his formal language, the latter "enriched" by pictograms, to be discussed below. But this only suggests the next question: How is the translation to be used?

Here we could resort to a defense of the method by an analogy, to which Lefebvre himself refers. Symbolic logic makes possible a translation of complex chains of conjunctions, disjunctions, negations, and implications into a formal symbolism, from which all "inessentials" have been eliminated. Inessentials are all those features of ordinary language that are irrelevant to the specific problem posed by logic, namely the problem of deducing a valid conclusion from a set of givens. The translation of propositions into chains of abstract symbols enables the logician to carry out operations far more complex than are possible in natural language. Thus, formal logic functions as a powerful machinery of deduction. Mathematics, by virtue of its abstract, highly *manipulable* symbolism functions in exactly the same way. In the mathematicized sciences, valid predictions are deduced from precisely stated assumptions that could not possibly be deduced using "common-sense" reasoning. Natural language cannot function in this way, first, because it is imprecise, second because in the grammars of natural language, syntactic, logical, semantic, and vaguely connotational aspects are tightly interlaced and quickly make any but the simplest chain of deductive reasoning hopelessly entangled.

Clearly, the impressive edifices of symbolic logic and of mathematics served as models for Lefebvre's algebra of reflexive polynomials and inspired the attempt at constructing a notation suitable for logical operations on the contents of the "inner worlds" of sentient, reflexive beings. His aim is to link up the subject matter of introspective (and interspective) psychology with the method of rigorous science. Whether this method (or others yet to appear on the path embarked upon by Lefebvre) can lead to achievements in psychology comparable, even to a very modest degree, to those made possible in natural science by mathematics, must at this time remain an open question. His demonstrations of the actual uses of the method, especially in problems involving conflict and cooperation expose his approach to severe criticism. Since I believe that in spite of some weaknesses in Lefebvre's exposition, his ideas are nevertheless important and deserving of sympathetic attention, I will try to show that these shortcomings do not seriously impair the import of the main message.

The Game Model of Conflict

The simplest example of a conflict is modeled by a game involving two players, each having a choice between two strategies (courses of action). The conflict is embodied in the different "utilities" that the players assign to the outcomes resulting from their choices. Suppose these utilities are represented by numbers, positive ones being gains, negative ones losses. If the sum of these utilities is zero, regardless of the outcome, this means that whatever one gains, the other loses. Such a game is called a zerosum game. It represents the most "severe" form of conflict, where the interests of the players are diametrically opposed. A game of this sort can be represented by a matrix, illustrated as Game 1:

	S_2	T_2
S_1	3, −3	−6, 6
T_1	−1, 1	5, −5

Game 1

The first player, called Row, chooses between the two horizontal rows, S_1 or T_1. The second player, called Column, chooses between the two vertical columns, S_2, or T_2. As the result of these choices, one of four outcomes obtains, $S_1 S_2$, $S_1 T_2$, $T_1 S_2$, or $T_1 T_2$. The two numbers in each cell of the matrix are the payoffs to Row and Column respectively. Since in this game their sum is always zero, Game 1 is a zerosum game.

A problem posed by game theory is how a "rational" player ought to choose. (A rational player is defined as one who tries to maximize his own payoff without regard for the payoff of the other.) Note that if Row were to choose first and if his choice were known to Column, Column would have no problem. If Row were to choose S_1, Column's rational choice is T_2; If Row were to choose T_1, Column's rational choice is S_2. Similarly, if Column were to choose first, Row would have no problem. However, if the choices must be made simultaneously or, equivalently, without knowledge of the other's choice, a real problem arises.

Suppose Row makes a *tentative* decision to choose T_1, say on the grounds that this choice will minimize his possible loss. Assuming that Column can "read Row's mind," Row will conclude that Column, on the basis of Row's tentative decision will (tentatively) decide to choose S_2. Now Row can reason further. On the basis of *that* tentative decision by Column, Row would be advised to choose S_1, so as to win 3. But if that is what he decides, Column, reading his thoughts, will choose T_2, in which case Row should choose T_1. And so on around and around. This is an example of infinite regression in the form "He thinks that I think that he thinks. . . ."

A principal achievement of game theory was that of finding an escape from this trap. By introducing the notion "expected utility" and of "mixed strategy," Von Neumann and Morgenstern (*Theory of Games and Economic Behaviour,* second edition, Princeton, N.J.: Princeton University Press, 1947) showed that every two-person zerosum game in matrix form has a "solution" in the sense of prescribing a strategy or a mixture of strategies to each player that can be naturally regarded as optimal under the constraints of the situation. Lefebvre refers to this solution on p. 56. It would seem, therefore, that all discussions about problems faced by opponents trying to "outguess" each other, at least in conflicts idealized as two-person zerosum games, are obsolete. Formally speaking, therefore, Lefebvre can be accused of trying to break through an open door when he discusses such problems at length (cf. pp. 112-126). In particular, the elaborate terminology distinguishing between "maps," "doctrines," and "decisions," and the corresponding symbolism (suggestive of multiplication and division but not related to these operations) appears superfluous.

As a rejoinder to this criticism, Lefebvre might point out that he is interested not in formal solutions of strategic problems but in reflexive analysis, which presumably singles out characteristically *psychological* aspects of these problems. Thus, one gains an advantage in conflict if one has an accurate image of the opponent's image of the situation and of how the opponent applies a particular "doctrine" in an attempt to solve the problem as *he* sees it; above all if one is able to *influence* the opponent's perception of the situation or his goals or his doctrine and at the same time conceal from him the fact that one *is* influencing him. The algebra of reflexive polynomials is introduced as an aid to this analysis. It may seem to the reader, however (at any rate it seems so to me) that Lefebvre's analysis is beset by some ambiguities. Bringing them to the surface may help to grasp his real meaning. Two examples will suffice, the representation and interpretation of the "all-seeing eye" and of the "mirror image of self" both in the context of two-person games.

The Case of the All-Seeing Eye

Lefebvre purports to show that in the context of a zerosum game, the conception of the opponent as an "all-seeing eye" leads an actor "to profess the maximin principle." The statement is ambiguous because there are two ways of inter-preting the maximin principle and two ways of interpreting the all-seeing eye. One way of defining the maximin principle is with reference to the actual strategies available in the game. Here a maximin strategy is one that maximizes the minimum payoff associated with each strategy. For example, in Game 1, Row has just two strategies, S_1 and T_1. The minimum payoff associated with S_1 is -6; that associated with T_1 is -1. Since $-1 > -6$, T_1 is Row's maximin strategy. Similarly, S_2 is Col-umn's maximin strategy. Another way of defining a maximin strategy is with reference to the space of "mixed" strategies generated by the set of original strategies. This conception will be elucidated below. Further, one way of defining an all-seeing eye is with reference to the thought processes of a player only. The "all-seeing eye" can read his opponent's thoughts and consequently "replicate" his decision process, but he cannot predict any arbitrary event, in particular an event determined by chance. Another way of defining an all-seeing eye is with reference to an ability to predict *all* future events.

Now let us understand by a maximin strategy one of the *given* strategies and by the all-seeing eye an opponent who can read thoughts but not predict chance events. Against such an opponent the maximin, as defined, is *not* the optimal choice. One can defend oneself against such an opponent by using a mixed strategy, i.e., letting a chance event choose one's strategy. In fact, in Game 1, if Row chooses his strategy by a random device that indicates S_1 with probability $2/5$ and T_1 with probability $3/5$, Row has an expected gain of $3/5$, which is larger than the pure maximin gain (-1).

This mixed strategy, denoted by $(2/5, 3/5)$ is also called the maximin. It is that with reference to the *entire set of mixed strategies,* each of which is defined by a corresponding probability vector. It is a maximin in the sense that it *guaran-tees* Row a minimum expected payoff *regardless* of what Column may do. We have seen that this (mixed) maximin is the best defense against the thought-reading all-seeing eye.

But now let us interpret the all-seeing eye as an opponent that can predict all events, in particular the outcome pre-scribed by the chance device. Or, if we want to stay in the context of thought-reading, let the all-seeing eye be aware of every *intended* action of the opponent. Now, even though the "decision" was made by the chance device, the carrying out of the decision is up to the player, which entails an intention, and this is read by the all-seeing eye. Against this all-seeing eye, the mixed strategy is not the best defense. The pure maximin, i.e., T_1 is the best Row can do.

I have examined this situation in some detail, because argu-ments of this sort have been advanced in connection with the so-called Newcomb's Paradox, in which the central problem concerns optimal decisions in a situation where one's thought processes are "monitored" by others. This idea is central also in this book. The ambiguities in Lefebvre's exposition are typical of many attempts to deal with such problems. In my opinion, they should be regarded as grist for the mill, stimu-lants of more rigorous and more refined analysis.

It is in this spirit that the old, now largely neglected, prob-lems of philosophy should be reexamined. In particular, the old free will vs. determinism paradox, which, in spite of hav-ing been exorcised by semantic philosophers, somehow will not go away. "Man can do what he will, but he cannot will what he will," wrote Schopenhauer. It is difficult to dismiss this proposition as "meaningless." One is tempted to ask whether, even if man can "will what he will," he can will what he "wills to will." It is the clumsiness of natural lan-guage that makes such multileveled concepts appear non-sensical. But we cannot be sure that they have no referent. I shall return to this point.

The Case of the Mirror Image

The so-called paradox of the Prisoner's Dilemma is well known to American readers interested in applications of game theory to psychology. Lefebvre uses a "degenerate" version of this game as another example of reflexive analysis. The illustrative story of the two gunmen is on page 66. The reader is invited to peruse it now.

Since Lefebvre does not say otherwise, we can assume that it makes no difference to either gunman whether the other dies or not, if he himself dies. Arbitrarily assigning a loss equivalent of ten rubles to getting killed, we can represent the situation as Game 2. Actually, the strategic structure of this game is the same, no matter what utility is assigned to being dead, as long as it is smaller than that associated with both gunmen surviving.

		Don't shoot	Shoot
S:	Don't shoot	0,0	−10, 1
T:	Shoot	1, −10	−10, −10

Game 2

Thus, each player is indifferent between "shoot" and "don't shoot" *if* the other shoots; but each player prefers to shoot if the other does *not* shoot. Therefore strategy T "weakly dominates" strategy S, and is the choice in accordance with the so-called "sure thing principle." Since both gunmen prefer staying alive to getting killed, each faces a dilemma.

In Lefebvre's illustration, each gunman sees the other as his exact mirror image. Not only whatever he does, the other does (like aiming the gun or lowering it), but also whatever one thinks, the other thinks. Thoughts "leak" through facial expressions; so that each realizes that his thought is instantaneously replicated by the other. Thus, when one gunman concludes that he must shoot, he realizes that the other has come to the same conclusion, and this decision appears "fatal." Changing his mind, the gunman lowers his gun and is aware of the other's identical decision. "Aha," he muses, "now I shall fool him and shoot." Immediately, a slight motion of the other's gun and a "sly expression" on his face signal the folly of *this* decision.

Actually, if each gunman were absolutely convinced that the other is a copy of himself, there would be no dilemma. For then the only two possible outcomes would be "both shoot" and "neither shoots." Since the latter outcome is preferred, and since the other is guaranteed to copy one's decision, the choice is clear: don't shoot. Nevertheless, according to Lefebvre, it is the mirror image model that leads to the dilemma.

Lefebvre explains this discrepancy by distinguishing between failure to shoot because one has *reached the decision* not to shoot and failure to shoot because one *has not arrived* at a decision. Here the psychological, rather than the formal decision-theoretic, aspect is brought out. In a formal decision-theoretic model, if "to shoot or not to shoot" are the only two alternatives posed, then failure to shoot is an indication that the latter alternative has been chosen and therefore, implicitly, that the actor has so decided. Clearly the psychological state of *indecision* has no place in this scheme. That the scheme is psychologically inadequate can be inferred from Hamlet's situation. The fact that Hamlet did not commit suicide does not mean that he has resolved his dilemma in favor to "to be."

It seems to me, however, that the discrepancy could be removed in a way more in accord with Lefebvre's own approach, if he had brought out with greater emphasis the difference between being equipped with a particular operator of awareness and *being aware* that one is so equipped, a distinction that he does mention in another context. (The resolution of the dilemma in terms of so-called theory of metagames derives from closely related ideas. The interested reader is referred to N. Howard, *Paradoxes of Rationality.*)

Next, Lefebvre concludes that if a gunman were equipped with an operator of awareness that dictates the maximin principle, he would not be in a dilemma. For him, the only

rational decision would be to shoot. Actually, a stronger conclusion is warranted. If a gunman were equipped with only
the "trivial" operator, $\omega=1$ (see p. 50) for the definition of
ω), that is, if he were aware only of the arena T, in this case
the game matrix, he would be compelled to shoot. For in
this case, the decision is dictated by the sure thing principle
(the choice of a dominating strategy), which is more compel-
ling than the maximin principle, derived from the awareness
of an opponent.

Another application of the mirror image model is to so-
called coordination games. Here the interests of the players
coincide, but can be realized only if the players can coordi-
nate their choices. This presents a problem if explicit communication is impossible. A simple example is the following
game: A coin is tossed, and two players are to guess the
outcome independently. If both guess the same outcome
(whether heads or tails), both get a prize; otherwise they
get nothing. In the absence of any "objective" reason for
guessing one way or another, coordination is impossible. If,
however, one guess is somehow "preferred," however slightly,
the mirror image model leads to a solution which not only
maximizes the probability of winning but actually guarantees
a win. Suppose, for example, one player thinks that heads is
slightly more likely to be guessed (by any one) than tails.
This is sufficient reason to choose heads, not merely in order
to increase the expectation of winning but actually to insure
winning. For the mirror image model leads to "I think that
he thinks that I will choose heads, and he thinks that I think
that he will choose heads." The solution hinges on the *belief*
that heads is a somewhat more probable choice and on the
assumption that the other also entertains this belief.

Experiments with this game have actually been performed
and showed that heads is indeed guessed with considerably
larger frequency than tails. The interesting thing is that when
"heads or tails" is played ordinarily in the sense of casting lots
to decide who will pay for drinks or who gets to play white
in chess, heads is chosen with only a slightly greater frequency

over tails. It is the knowledge or even the *supposition* that this is the case that suffices to turn a slight majority into a substantial majority in the coordination game.

Coordination games have been discussed in a large variety of contexts by T. C. Schelling (1960). Lefebvre errs in suggesting that Schelling's analysis does not go far enough. He assumes that Schelling's solution requires that the "focal point" at which coordination takes place has some "objective" advantage for both players, as, for instance, when each tries to find the other in a park when it is raining, and each decides that the pavillion is the most likely place of meeting. In one of Schelling's examples, a man and his wife who lost each other in a crowded department store both cheerfully head for the lost and found. Unlike the pavillion, this spot has no "objective" advantage. The choice depends on a shared sense of humor and on the knowledge that the sense of humor is shared.

Since Lefebvre introduces his reflexive polynomials as (among the other things) a tool of strategic analysis, it is fair to ask whether this formalism sheds any new light on strategic problems as such. In my opinion, it does not. In deductive power, the language of reflexive polynomials does not compare with that of the mathematics of game theory, which provides *formal* solutions (in the sense of prescribing optimal strategies) at least to all two-person zerosum matrix games. Moreover, the methods of game theory have been extended to much more complex strategic problems, such as so-called infinite games (games of timing, games of pursuit and evasion, games of dual control, etc.) by means of a mathematical apparatus far more powerful than the one introduced by Lefebvre. True, the methods used in solving two-person zerosum games fail for various reasons when attempts are made to extend them to nonzerosum games (where the interests of the players clash only partly) and to games with more than two players (where coalitions are possible). But the very reasons for the failure, when thoroughly analyzed, lead to a plethora of new concepts and important insights into the nature of "rational" (i.e., strategic) conflict and into the very nature of "rationality," revealing complexities and nuances that remain hidden if the intuited notion of rationality is accepted as sufficiently clear. This new conceptual repertoire, generated by the analysis of nonzerosum and n-person games remains beyond the scope of this book.

Perhaps, however, it is not fair to compare Lefebvre's approach with that of game theory, since strategic analysis is only one area where he attempts to apply his apparatus. As he states at the outset, his primary interest is psychology and the primary function of his formalism is that of reintroducing (on a rigorous basis) the introspective and interspective mode of investigation into psychology. On that score, we must examine the potential contribution of his method to psychology rather than to the theory of rational decision, which is the domain of game theory.

Lefebvre starts with pointing out the inadequacies of behaviorist psychology, in particular, the impossibility of realizing its program of eliminating mental phenomenology as an object of investigation in its own right. I find myself in full agreement with his critique. At the same time, I believe Lefebvre shares my conviction that once the "scientification" of a discipline has set in, there is no going back. Like any other discipline purporting to expand human knowledge regarding any phenomenological realm, psychology must develop as a science. The limitations of behaviorism stem from the narrowness of its conceptual base, not from its insistence on adhering to scientific standards of cognition. Lebebvre may even agree that behaviorism has made an important contribution to the maturation of psychology as a science by insisting on the primacy of the experiment as a last court of appeal in disputes about the "truth" of a theory. If so, then it behooves us to examine the potentialities of Lefebvre's approach to experimental psychology.

Suggested Links with
Experimental Psychology

Experimental studies of what Lefebvre calls "reflexive control" are presented in Chapter 6. The experiments cited show that a rigidly programmed automaton can "outplay" a naive human subject in a simple game. The automaton "feints" by exhibiting a pattern of behavior and in this way supposedly induces in the subject an assumption regarding its "strategy." Then the pattern is switched, so that the subject makes the wrong moves. By the time the subject catches on (if he does), the pattern changes again. The average subject does not "catch up" with the automaton and consequently "loses."

Besides being a demonstration of a very simple case of reflexive control (influence over another's thought processes), these experiments suggest some avenues of research. To begin with, the principles underlying this type of automata (which Lefebvre and his co-workers call "dribblings") are different from those governing other, vastly more sophisticated game-playing automata, such as chess-playing computers. The strategies built into the latter are incomparably more complex, but they are not designed to influence the opponent's thought processes. The chess-playing computer plays the board, not the opponent. That is, it selects (according to prescribed criteria of evaluation) the "best possible move" regardless of *who* plays against it, that is, regardless of the other's style of play. A chess-playing dribbling would attempt to play the opponent as well as the board. That is, it would guide its strategies by utilizing the thought processes of the opponent *induced* in the opponent by the dribbling. Many chess masters do just this or at least guide their strategies by deduced thought processes of the particular opponent. To be sure, the program built into Lefebvre's dribbling was fixed and used against all subjects, even in different games. However, the selection of that program, was made on the basis of a preliminary pilot experiment. It was chosen as the most likely to "outplay" the average naive subject. The "next generation" of dribblings may well be tailored to individual opponents or will modify their strategy on the basis of the opponent's manifested predilections. In fact, dribblings that beat human opponents in simple hide-and-guess games have been constructed in the United States. But the line of *psychological* research suggested by these machines has not been pursued, namely, in search of answers to the following questions: Is it possible, and, if so, how to induce certain thought patterns in a human subject and to exploit them whether or not the subject anticipates such manipulations? Under what conditions is reflexive control facilitated or inhibited? How does one effectively defend oneself against it?

Realization of the import of such questions pervades this book. (They fall, outside the scope of mathematical game theory since game-theoretic models are completely "de-psychologized" in the sense that complete rationality of players is typically assumed throughout.) Such questions are also central in attempts to design sophisticated strategies of bargaining and negotiation. While the utilitarian aspects of such attempts may be questionable (to the extent that whatever can be learned by one side, can be learned by other), their relevance and import to psychology is, in my opinion considerable. Lefebvre deserves credit for emphasizing the salience of these phenomena.

How much reflexive polynomials can be of help in pursuing this direction of research is another matter. There is an apparently "unbridgeable abyss," to use Lefebvre's expression in another context, between the almost trivially simple experimental illustrations of the notion of reflexive control and the realization of a full experimental program guided by models suggested by reflexive polynomials. The problem, to which I see no solution, is that of finding a point of contact between the symbolism and observations. Lefebvre's personae are introduced together with their operators of awareness, but nowhere is a procedure suggested, however crude, that might make the nature of these operators manifest even in a particular situation, let alone as a more or less stable characteristic of a real person. Moreover, even if such suggestions were at hand, it is one thing to suggest a procedure and quite another to carry it out and get a meaningful result.

The difficulty is illustrated dramatically in attempts to get at much more clearly defined "characteristics" of individuals to serve as indices of their mental states, for example utilities registered on an interval scale assigned to objects or subjective probabilities assigned to possible events. Operational definitions of these concepts prescribe perfectly definite experimental procedures for determining the corresponding psychological characteristics. However, formal mathematical analysis also identifies the criteria that must be satisfied by the data obtained in these experiments in order for a utility scale or a probability measure characterizing a given individual *to exist at all.* Essentially, these are certain criteria of consistency in decision-making. The sad fact of life confronting the experimenting psychologist, however, is that people are typically *not* consistent even in apparently similar situations, even in replications of what seems to be the same situation. To be sure, just because psychological parameters are terribly elusive, the search for them need not be given up. It is only unfortunate that in the process of identifying these parameters via formal theoretical or mathematical deduction, one tends to lose sight of the formidable difficulties of tracking them down in reality.

A case in point is the coefficient β_0, the "coefficient of empathy," linking the internal utilities of one persona to the external utilities of another. In suggesting a way of determining this parameter (cf. p. 152) Lefebvre by-passes the question of whether the procedure can be reasonably expected to "catch" what he intends to catch, something, which by definition of a parameter remains invariant in a given class of situations. Yet this *is* the central problem of experimental psychology (whether behavioral or mentalistic): the determination of parameters in terms of which observations can be explained or (one hopes) predicted. While this problem remains unsolved, the theory remains without even a prospect of an empirical foundation. It seems useless, therefore, to "build" on these nonexistent foundations, for instance to superimpose successive orders of internal utilities ("I attach a value of his evaluation of my values . . .") or to generalize the model to a whole society where the empathy coefficients must be determined for each pair of individuals.

It is easy to dismiss formulations of this sort as futile exercises. Yet it is extremely difficult to draw the line between a substantive theory and sterile formalism. At one extreme are the beady-eyed empiricists, who dismiss any theoretical formulation that does not immediately pay off in the hard currency of corroborating data. At the other are starry-eyed metaphysicists, for whom the only criteria of validity of any speculation is their own belief that it makes sense and reveals some "truth." In the middle are those who command the techniques of formal deduction (e.g., mathematics), appreciate the value of pursuing these deductions to *formally* valid theoretical consequences, and recognize in principle the necessity of empirical corroboration, but take on varying degrees of responsibility for translating their findings into hypotheses that are verifiable in actuality, not merely in imagination.

This "middle" is very broad, and it is difficult to choose a tenable position on this spectrum. The point is that even purely formal investigations with no discernible connections to data sometimes lead to important insights. The "philosophical" offshoots of game theory have been mentioned. Another area, somewhat related "in spirit" to the central theme of this book is mathematical linguistics. N. Chomsky posed the problem of finding a suitable mathematical model of a grammar. A model in this sense would be a collection of formal rules governing the concatenation of linguistic units (phonemes, morphemes, or such) into sequences that are acceptable sentences in a given language. The rules will constitute a grammar if by applying them purely mechanically (as a computer would) one can generate *all* possible sentences in the given language and if no sequence will be generated that is not acceptable as a sentence.

Since no rigid limitations can be imposed on the length of a sentence, the totality of acceptable sequences is potentially infinite. This in itself does not preclude the formulation of a grammar with a finite number of rules, because the rules can be recursive. However, as Chomsky has shown, certain *classes* of rules, for example those that are representable by a finite automaton (an automaton with a finite number of states), cannot produce an indefinite number of sentences having a certain structure. In particular, such finite automata cannot produce sentences with unlimited "imbedding" of phrases within phrases.

To cite an example of Chomsky's, "This is obvious" is an acceptable English sentence. "That this is obvious is obvious" is also grammatically correct. "That this is obvious is obvious is obvious" sounds almost incomprehensible and would not be written or spoken by any one with a sense of linguistic propriety. Nevertheless, the last sequence does not violate English grammar in a way that can be pinpointed. That it is not nonsense can be seen from the following "concretization" of its meaning: "It was clear to everyone that the obviousness of his remarks was immediately apparent."

From the fact that the rules of English grammar make it possible (in principle) to keep inbedding phrases within phrases and from the fact that a finite automaton cannot generate such unlimited imbeddings, Chomsky concludes that other models of grammar must be sought and goes on to examine "more powerful" models.

Now from the empirical point of view, the theoretical conclusion that "English cannot be generated by a finite automaton" is meaningless. Even though *in principle* no limitation can be placed on the length of English sentences, *in actuality* there is a length that no English sentence ever spoken or written or any that will *ever* be spoken or written can exceed, if only because human life is finite. Aside from that, the limitations of human memory and attention preclude more than very few imbeddings of the sort mentioned, perhaps no more than five or six, or, to be wildly liberal, twenty, in any context. Of what use, then, is a theory of grammar that starts with the assumption that unlimited imbeddings are permissible?

The answer to this question is that the theory of grammar developed by mathematical tools is not directed toward immediate applications to concrete linguistic data. Its product is insight into what *kinds* of rules can generate what kinds of (idealized) grammars. In other words, the end product of this theory is not a description or a prediction of linguistic events but rather the creation of a conceptual repertoire, a framework of thought in which to develop theories of language structure.

Perhaps Lefebvre's reflexive polynomials should be approached from a similar point of view. As verifiable models of human behavior they are certainly not promising. The chains "I think that he thinks. . . ." or "I know that he doesn't know that I know. . . ." or "I am glad that he is glad that I am sad. . . ." etc. are treated as potentially infinite. In practice they must be severely limited even though no definite cut-off point for the reflexive process can be suggested. Confining oneself to finite chains does not help either. The prospect of characterizing real human individuals by specific reflexive polynomials, even in strictly circumscribed situations must, I am afraid, remain a fantasy. If, however, theoretical conclusions could be drawn from models of this sort that perforce necessitate the introduction of new concepts or new ways of looking at human psychology, the efforts will have been worthwhile.

Philosophical Implications

There is no question that to the author of this book the methods described therein have been richly suggestive. The range of topics that he somehow connects to the central theme is very broad. For the most part, the ideas echo the prevalent philosophical, especially epistemological speculations of our age. As in every other age, the prominent philosophical questions are those that reflect ideological commitments and these, in turn, stem from the broad alignments in social conflicts. In this regard, Marx was right: An ideological commitment is a rationalization of a position in social conflict. Where his vulgarizers adumbrated this insight was in making it appear that there is only one essential conflict, overshadowing all others, that it stems exclusively from the way the "capitalist system" works, and that victory on the global scale is assured to one side only by submission to a militarily organized elite, which is in possession of a "science" wherein the "laws of motion" of human society have been discovered.

There are, in fact, many social conflicts, and the "fronts" are complex and criss-crossed. In our age, these fronts emerge and shift rapidly, because the rate of social change must now be measured by decades instead of centuries. Since decades are spanned by the memory of a single generation, the shifting fronts are highly visible and so induce intense preoccupation with philosophical questions.

Two such questions are presently at the forefront of attention:

1. Is a social science possible, and, if so, what ought to be its epistemological base?

2. What is or ought to be man's relation to nature?

Both questions were generated by the impact of megatechnology on our lives. The first is prompted by the perceived discrepancy between man's power over nature and his helplessness in the face of formidable social problems. The second stems from the threats of the population explosion, the depletion of natural resources, and the degradation of the environment.

Suggested answers to these questions reflect distinct ideological commitments. Answers to the first question, divide those who accept power as an effective organizing principle in human society and those who reject it. This division is not according to whether one believes or does not believe in the possibility of a social science (believers and unbelievers are found in both camps). The division is on the issue of the epistemological underpinnings. For those who accept the power principle and believe in "social science," an extension of natural science epistemology to phenomena involving human acting and thinking seems natural. They argue that since man has achieved mastery over his natural environment by the tools of natural science, he can achieve mastery over the social environment by applying these tools to the study of human behavior. The key word in this profession of faith is "mastery." Implicitly, science is identified with technology. Mastery of environment is knowing how to manipulate it, whether the objects manipulated are raw materials or masses of human beings or opponents in strategic conflict. "Social engineering" is practised (or believed by the authorities to be practised) in totalitarian states. In societies where competitive acquisition is promoted to a way of life, large areas of "social science" are geared to developing effective means of competition. In micro-economics, the firm and its goals are at the center of interest. Pragmatically oriented "political science" is concerned with factors influencing elections, with the distribution and the use of power in legislative and administrative bodies, with strategic uses of power in international relations, and so on. An investigator with this orientation invariably assumes the position of a single actor (although, in the interest of objectivity, the actor may be arbitrarily selected) with whom he identifies during the investigation. Other actors with their mentalities or goals may enter the picture but only in order to take into account the obstacles in the way of achieving the central actor's goals.

Those who reject the power principle see the problems of social science in a different perspective. Here the picture of an actor manipulating his environment dissolves, since other actors are no longer submerged as parts of the environment but appear as beings comparable to the central actor or, indeed, to the investigator. In particular, a psychology that by-passes the problem of constructing the "inner worlds" of sentient beings or believes them to be deducible from observed physiological states appears inadequate. A sociology or a political science that ignores the effect of "knowing" the state of a system or the effect of publishing what one knows on that very state seems to neglect the most important distinction between the natural and the social sciences, one that has profound implications for the methodology of the latter.

Answers to the second question also reflect different attitudes to the concept of power. In seeing himself as a "master," lording over nature, instead of a part of nature, man may find that his power is illusory. That is, in regarding nature as a manipulable object, man may have prepared his own demise.

An approach that ascribes "reality" (in its own right) to inner worlds, one's own and others' has far-reaching implications not only in the context of abstruse metaphysical, or epistemological or theological speculations but also for concrete methodological problems in psychology and sociology and even for practical problems arising in public policy and in international relations.

Consider the following question in developmental psychology: How does a small child internalize the meaning of the verb "to think?" Facile explanations in terms of associating sounds with things or events via conditioning are hardly satisfactory. "Thinking" is experienced "from the inside," not as a part of the external environment. Yet the four-year-old gives ample evidence of knowing intuitively the full "meaning" of this term, which has no external referents. To take another example, how is a one-year-old child able to imitate? I touch my nose; it touches its nose. I close my eyes, it does the same. How does it know that my nose and eyes are analogues of its nose and eyes? In India there is a superstition that prohibits showing a mirror to a baby. Unless I am shown experimental evidence to the contrary, I assume that an Indian baby can imitate as well as any other.

Next consider the concept of the self-realizing or self-negating predictions embodied in the principle, "In human affairs,

an image of a situation influences the situation." The working of the principle in runs on banks, crises, panics, etc. is
well known. Questions have been raised whether publication
of preelection polls ought not be made illegal. (If I am not
mistaken, it is illegal in some countries.) In North America,
expected numbers of traffic fatalities are published immediately before long summer weekends in the hope that publications of these figures will help reduce the actual number.

The complex ethical questions relating to euthanasia and
abortion that are now subjects of intense public discussion
cannot be resolved one way or another without involving the
concept of the other's "inner world," that is, the "thou"
distinguished from, yet on another level of awareness also
identified with, the "I." Answers to the above questions stem
essentially from assumptions about the existence or non-
existence of the "thou."

Finally consider the *psychological* question related to the
ethical aspect of the "I-thou" relation. What is the origin of
the "ego" and of its extension by projection to other sentient
beings? In the paradigm of positivist science, there seems to
be no way to formulate this question as a *problème bien
posé*. It must remain in the philosophical mode. Yet to dismiss it as a "pseudo-question" in the way characteristic of
a hard-nosed positivist position seems somehow wrong. In
spite of the impossibility of answering this question in a way
supported by "hard evidence," it is difficult to get rid of
the feeling that the question makes sense. All of us know
(internally) the meaning of "myself." Most of us will deny
the existence of this knowledge in living things "below" a
certain level of evolutionary development (from our necessarily anthropomorphic point of view). We feel, therefore,
if we believe in evolution, that there must have been a time
when the perception of the "ego" emerged. Lefebvre conjec-
tures that it emerged on the basis of an "external surrogate,"
registered by *the other* (the "thou") in a primitive social
situation. The conjecture is, to say the least, intriguing. It
seems to make good sense. It is also challengeable, therefore

it is grist for the philosophical mill and should be welcomed by anyone who values creative philosophy.

The concept of ego-awareness as a prerequisite of "adequate reflection of reality" is manifested in humble folk wisdom. I remember a children's story, probably of ancient ancestry, about the adventures of a boy in the land of simpletons. He meets a group of them engaged in a heated discussion. Asking what the trouble is, the boy is told that one of the group vanished mysteriously. "We were ten when we started out," says the spokesman, "but now we are nine. We have lost a comrade and cannot find him." "Let me see you count," says the boy. Each one, in turn, counts and gets nine (intersubjective validation!), because he does not count himself. When the boy explains the source of their error, they are grateful and confer on him the title of "wise." In this way Silly Billy, as he was known, becomes Wise William.

Here is another example, closer to "scientific" psychology, taken from Piaget's experiments on concept formation in children. A boy, who is known to have one brother is asked whether he has a brother. The answer is yes. He is then asked whether his brother has a brother. Below a certain average age, the answer is no. The identification of "I" with "my brother's brother" has not yet crystallized.

I discuss these questions at some length to emphasize their central importance (as it seems to me) in psychology, in philosophy, particularly in ethics, and even in politics.

One area where the ideas embodied in "reflexive phenomenology" have made little headway is international relations, dominated by "realist" conceptions. To be sure, lip service is paid to the paradoxical features of some nonzerosum games, to the importance of images and their interactions, and even to self-realizing assumptions (for instance in escalating arms races). But a "realist" policy continues to be based on the concept of a central actor, pursuing "national interests" via acting or exerting influence upon *others*. The dependence of the presumed underlying "reality" (the interaction of national interests) upon the self-perpetuating *perception* of reality as it is depicted in the "realist" model does not enter the picture.

In short, ontology, dealing with questions of existence and reality, and epistemology, dealing with questions concerning the source of our knowledge, pervade not only traditional philosophy but all facets of human life. The particular positions taken on these questions depends largely on one's ideological commitments and, in turn, provides a framework for formulating them. In his society, Lefebvre took a heretical position on these questions. Lenin himself had warned against seeking a conciliation between the "idealist" and the "materialist" positions in philosophy. He deplored "the innumerable endeavors to 'transcend' the 'onesidedness' of materialism and idealism," which is just what Lefebvre is endeavoring to do in this book. Lefebvre rejects the *tertium non datur* of official Soviet philosophy: "Either materialism consistent to the end, or the falsehood and confusion of idealism—that is the alternative." Lefebvre attempts a synthesis (cf. p. 170).

Regarding some questions, Lefebvre stands on Marxist positions, as when he projects the origin of human language, hence the very "humanness" of man upon cooperative, synchronized, and differentiated labor. He even projects the origin of high order analogies (precursors of language) to the use of tools, that is to human work activity, for instance by suggesting that the holistic concept of a "river" had its origin in experience with ropes. Again the conjecture is grist for the philosophical mill. My cat has no symbolic language and has never worked with tools, yet gives evidence of a faculty for forming high order analogies. As I shave, she jumps on the sink and seems to be fascinated by the sight of water going down the drain. For some time after the water has gone, she sits motionless, apparently watching the hole. Can it be that she has internalized the analogy "water-mouse; drain-hole?" Or would Lefebvre say that although she can analogize, she does not have a denotative language, because she does not work with tools?

All this is anthropomorphising, of course, condemned by behaviorist psychology as "unscientific." But how can any person unafraid to use his imagination avoid it? The problem is where to draw the line. Lefebvre, evidently draws no line and carries anthropomorphic analogy all the way to the universe.

In evaluating the author's excursions into abstruse metaphysical regions, one should keep in mind the tremendous emphasis placed on the "fundamental tenets" of materialist philosophy in Soviet education. I suspect that even those who have emancipated themselves from the catechism still feel the need to anchor themselves firmly to some metaphysical foundation. On the other hand, the book is pervaded with attempts to anchor a world view in concepts emerging in the exact sciences and mathematics. This tendency Lefebvre shares with many Western writers who bring into the philosophy of the social sciences ideas distilled (as it appears to them) from thermodynamics, quantum theory, relativity theory, information theory, game theory, foundations of mathematics, topology, etc., etc. These allusions often make a poor impression on those who have technical knowledge of these matters. Attempts to deal with them in the philosophical mode, un-reinforced by the rigorous and complex mathematical apparatus that brought these ideas into being in the first place, usually betray naiveté and are frequently pervaded by gross errors. For this reason, Lefebvre's disclaimer to the effect that he is only "playing" at constructing theories, not actually trying to construct them, should be taken literally. In particular, his discussion of cosmology should be read as one would read a science fiction fantasy. Some may find these speculations intriguing.

The use of iconic signs in connection with reflexive polynomials is a more serious attempt at methodological innovation. Its advantages, however, escape me completely. Granted that it might be desirable to introduce a systematic notation for expressing the emotive content of "texts," I fail to see the purpose of performing "algebraic operations" on cartoon faces. It would be another matter if one could somehow ascertain the transformations that these images undergo as they are "assimilated" and "reflected." Then one could argue that because gestalts are often more efficient carriers of information than sequences of abstract analytic units, something could be gained. But here the expressions are put on the faces by the investigator who draws them. They have no life of their own. As they are presently conceived, they can at best serve as means of recording an investigator's attitudes toward the objects of his investigation. It is not clear how mixing the analytic-formal and the expressive-impressionistic modes of notation will help put psychology on new foundations.

Two concretely "scientific" contributions are offered in this book. One is a formal notation to register the extent to which in a given situation a number of actors "assimilate" or "replicate" each other's inner worlds and the underlying reality. The other is an experimental method designed to assess the possibilities of "inducing" in subjects certain hypotheses with the view of "exploiting" them in a game of strategy. The rest is philosophy, ranging from reformulations of millenium-old questions to free-wheeling speculations.

The reflexive polynomial notation was clearly inspired by the author's "crooked mirror" paradigm of human cognition (cf., p. 45). It could *conceivably* be of help if one had models, however crude, of the distortions impressed by the mirrors on the images in some specific situations or classes of situations. Then the author's attempt to "breathe life" into the abstract symbols by introducing iconic signs might have a basis of justification.

The experiments are clearly related to problems involved in designing game-playing machines. The added feature of "reflexive control" is, to my knowledge, new.

The "philosophy" should be read as philosophy, that is, as exercises in flexing intellectual muscles after taking a heavy draught of a heady drink called "imagination." What distinguishes contemporary efforts of this sort from traditional philosophy is the dramatic impact of science and of global social problems on our lives, felt by every intellectually active person. The traditional philosophical questions like "What is the nature of reality?" "How do we know what we know?" "What are the origins of consciousness, of language of the ego, of empathy, of the 'oceanic feeling' " keep recurring, but we are almost compelled to put them into perspectives opened up by science. Social reality puts at the forefront of attention the phenomena of alienation (which in Lefebvre's terms would, perhaps, be represented by hermetic isolation of "inner worlds"); the phenomenon of brain washing (represented by his models of "reflexive control"); the phenomenon of self-realizing prophesies (modeled by introducing subjective features into games of strategy); the phenomenon of the tragedy of the commons (pinpointing the reflexive aspects of social responsibility), and many others. It may be especially interesting to American readers to see how these phenomena are interpreted philosophically by a thinker who was reared in a social milieu radically different from ours but who reaches out to a global intellectual community.

—Anatol Rapoport

INTRODUCTION

The scientific outlook, as it crystallized in the first half of our century, was based on two tacit assumptions. The first, expressed apocryphally, says: "A theory entertained by an investigator about some object is not a product of that object's activity." The second says: "The object does not depend on the circumstance that a theory reflecting that object exists."

The first postulate registers the investigator's dominant position vis-a-vis the object: There are no objects that surpass the investigator, which enable him to discover his goals and to help or hinder him in realizing them. One way of expressing this postulate is to say that nature is neither benevolent nor malevolent. The second postulate enables the investigator to speak of properties of laws inherent in objects These are assumed to exist objectively and are only registered by the investigator.

If, on the other hand, we admit that a scientific conception may influence an object, then a theory that reflects some regularity may change this regularity and so may falsify itself. This situation is not the same as that in quantum physics. There the findings obtained by the investigator depend upon or are even the results of interactions between the object and the investigator's apparatus; but the findings do not influence the properties of the physical process which they reflect. Thus, Planck's constant does not depend on the fact that it was published. The scientific conception, not being a physical event, is not a property of the apparatus.

The abovementioned postulates arose in the context of physical investigations. The study of mental phenomena has a long history in which teleological, psychiatric, and specifically scientific lines of thought crossed. The end of the last and the beginning of the present century were characterized by attempts to turn psychology into a science. The most successful disciplines, especially physics, were to serve as models.

The nature of mental phenomena is fundamentally different from that of physical phenomena. Whereas the "given" confronting the physicist is the huge brilliant world of things, the "given" of the psychologist is the dark internal world, ethereal and difficult to capture. Directing his sight inward, the psychologist attempts to represent this "given" by special concepts which, when synthesized (successfully or otherwise), appear to him as "mental phenomena." This process has been called introspection. The work of the psychologist then consists in projecting this result of introspection upon other thinking and feeling beings.

The other's inner world is concealed from the investigator. He observes only behavior. However, to the extent that his own behavior is generated by his own psyche, the psychologist complements his objective observations of the other's behavior by the other's psyche. Such is the mechanism of the psychologist's work. Different schools of psychology offered different justifications for this mechanism, but it was always present.

The first decades of our century saw a radical change in the direction of psychological research, namely, a conscious turning away from the introspective method. In the United States E. L. Thorndyke proposed to abandon all attempts at introspective analysis and to undertake an investigation of the "actual givens" of behavior. The behaviorist approach carried the promise of making psychology scientific. It instigated the notion of the "black box" with the stimuli as inputs and responses as outputs, both of which can be registered and measured. The problem of psychology became that of discovering the functional connections between stimuli and responses. The entire field of "mental phenomenology" remained outside the realm of scientific analysis.

There is a remarkable contradiction in the behaviorist scheme. Quite clearly the response of the subject is to a considerable degree determined by meaning. But a text obtains a meaning only in the inner worlds of the subject and the experimenter. Therefore, in order to clarify just what is a stimulus, the experimenter must turn to his own inner world, that is, perform an introspective act. Moreover, he must suppose that the meaning is understood by the subject, that is, he must perform a projective act—attribute a psyche to the subject.

The "stimulus-response" scheme, having castrated psychology, does not permit the experimenter to take note even of such an ordinary occurrence as a deception perpetrated by the subject during an experiment, since this requires the experimenter to penetrate into the subject's inner world, which is forbidden. Thus the proscription of introspection either leads to a dead end or to a camouflaged utilization of it, that is, to self-deception.

Besides behaviorism, there were attempts to by-pass introspection by way of investigating regularities in the functioning of the brain. However, here, too, there is no way of avoiding introspection. The point is that physiological states must be interpreted. For instance, it is not possible to register pain by any apparatus. It is only possible to measure some physical parameter which the experimenter can interpret as "pain." In doing so, the experimenter must refer to his own unique inner world. Thus, resorting to physiology does not remove the necessity of an independent approach to mental phenomena. We are simply led back to the classical philosophical problem of the relation between mind and matter.

The way in which concepts of mind and matter were combined was always determined by the intellectual techniques of a given society. At times, there were models based on the part-whole relationships; at other times models based on the notion of "penetration" and other relationships, rather simplistic from a modern point of view. These models tended to establish a subordination of the one to the other. An example: "Although the soul has no form, it acquires (as light does) the extent and the form of the body in which it lives" (Chatterjee and Datta, 1954). In other areas we now have more sophisticated techniques of speculation. Many philosophical problems have been revived and have created their own disciplines. For instance, the perennial question of whether the universe is finite or infinite is now examined in the context of relativity theory. Discussions of this problem in the language of "common sense" are no longer effective. The problem of the relation between mind and matter, however, has a different status. For the modern engineer the very existence of mental phenomenology is far from obvious. For him the only existing events are those that can be at least potentially accommodated in behavioral schemes. The triumph of cybernetics is not limited to the appearance of new effective methods of analyzing complex systems; it portends also a radical narrowing of the ontological field within which the problems of scientific analysis must be confined.

It is amusing to note that the question of whether artifacts can be equipped with minds has been turned into the question of whether machines can think and that this question was answered by Turing in the best behaviorist tradition. Evidently one of the principal methodological problems in the investigation of complex systems is that of developing models of reality in which structural relations between mental and physical phenomenology can be established. Depending on how the problem is solved, we shall either be able to view systems as entities "endowed with intellect" or will have to content ourselves with two unconnected approaches and formalize our capitulation as a principle analogous to Bohr's principle of complementarity (Bohr, 1955).

In this book, we shall try to sketch some approaches that may be useful for integrating the two directions of research.

We conclude that in research on complex systems, mental phenomenology cannot be dispensed with or by-passed. But in admitting mental phenomenology, the investigator admits the existence of objects comparable or even superior to himself; because, having objectivized mental phenomena, he must recognize various "intensities" of these phenomena. He has no basis for putting himself at the pinnacle of this scale of intensity. In this way, he is led to reject the two postulates of the natural scientific outlook.

The contrasting juxtaposition of object and investigator appears justified only when the objects are not endowed with psyche. When they are so endowed, the relation between the investigator and the object becomes a relation between two investigators, each of whom is an object for the other (Lefebvre, 1969a).

The relations between objects-investigators manifest themselves most clearly in conflicts. For this reason, conflict is of interest in the study of interactions between an investigator and a system comparable to or superior to himself. It becomes vitally necessary to penetrate into the opponent's plans, that is, to analyze his thought processes. The very situation itself forces each participant in a conflict to investigate the inner world of his opponent and to construct an appropriate theory. This is an unusual interrelation between an object and a theory about it. The object constantly tries to "escape" from the theory, that is, to falsify it.

In studying social-psychological phenomena the investigator becomes one of the personae in a specific game, which we shall call a *reflexive* game. To the extent that the investigator cannot exclude the possibility of contact with the other personae studied, his theoretical constructions, being assimilated by those other personae, may change radically the behavior of the whole system. On the other hand, the researcher may find himself a prisoner of his object: His conception may be imposed on him by the object. Apparently, reflexive relations between object-investigators ought to be subjected to a special kind of analysis.

Reflexion in its traditional philosophic-psychological sense is the ability to assume the role of an observer, or of an investigator, or of a controller of one's own body, actions or thoughts. We shall extend this meaning to include the ability to become an investigator of another's actions and thoughts. This generalized meaning enables us to construct an integrated area of research; to single out the reflexive process as a special phenomenon that determines the specifics of interrelations between objects and investigators.

We shall introduce an algebraic method that will enable us to examine the mechanics of conscious phenomena apart from their content, although content is usually viewed as an inseparable attribute of consciousness. In examining the structure of "the conscious," that is, reflexive structures, we can view the image and consciousness as separate categories and so study the phenomenon of "the conscious" separated from its psychological substrate.

A similar separation was effected in logic when investigations of "laws of thought" as such became possible. In pursuing the study of logic we need not answer the question, "What is mind?" Nor do we have to answer this question in studying the reflexive process. However, this remains one of the most important questions relating to science in general. In the past two thousand years hardly any progress has been made toward understanding how mental phenomena are connected to physiological and physical reality. At any rate, we find no place for mental phenomena in the physicalist picture of the world.

Chapter 1

AN ALGEBRA OF

REFLEXIVE PROCESSES

Imagine a room full of crooked mirrors like those in amusement parks. The mirrors are placed at different angles. Let a pencil be dropped. Its fall will be fantastically reflected in the mirrors, and the reflexions will also be reflected. Thus, the trajectory, already distorted in the various mirrors, will be further distorted in the avalanche of multiply reflected images. A reflexive system can be thought of as a system of mirrors and the multitude of reflexions in them. Each mirror represents a "persona" characterized by a particular position. The vastly complex flow of reflexions represents the reflexive process.

The example illustrates the difference between a physical process and a social-psychological one. The trajectory of the pencil is a physical process; the entire flow of reflexions is a social-psychological one.

Imagine now an observer entering this room. (He, too, is a mirror.) The situation has changed fundamentally. Each movement of the investigator is accompanied by a continual change in the multiple reflexions.

At times we shall speak of an external observer, supposing that he is not reflected in the mirrors (personae) investigated by him.

We shall introduce an apparatus designed for analyzing reflexive processes (Lefebvre, 1965a; 1967; 1972; 1977). Human conflict will serve as the concrete context of which this apparatus will be a particular schematization. The use of the apparatus, however, is not limited to conflict situations. Such situations are merely the clearest illustrations of reflexive processes.

Representation of Reflexive Systems

The conflicting parties will be represented by X, Y, and Z. In order to make a decision, X must construct a model of the situation, say schematize an arena in which armies will interact. Similarly, Y must also construct a model. Besides, Y may be aware that X has a model of the situation. Z, in turn, may be aware that the inner worlds of X and Y are structured in a particular way. Success in conflict depends largely on the way the conflicting parties conceive each other's inner worlds. In order to interpret correctly the actions of an opponent, one must take into account the opponent's reflexive constructions. For instance, a shift of forces in the arena may serve to solve some actual tactical problem; but it may also be a maneuver calculated to be taken into account by the opponent who will make his decision on the basis of his interpretation.

In Figure 1.1 the arena is represented by a rectangle, the three personae (parties) by three circles. Suppose at time t_1 X became aware of the situation. This means that a representation of the arena has formed inside him. In Figure 1.2 the picture represented in Figure 1.1 has been inserted into

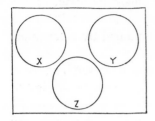

Figure 1.1

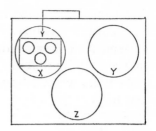

Figure 1.2

X. The situation has now changed: New elements have appeared in it. Next, at time t_2, Y has become aware of the new situation. To represent the resulting situation, we have to reproduce the picture represented in Figure 1.2 inside Y (cf., Figure 1.3). If, at time t_3, Z became aware of this situation, we should have to insert everything represented in

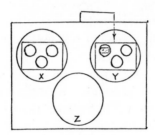

Figure 1.3

Figure 1.3 into Z. Besides being difficult for typographical reasons, it would be extremely inconvenient to operate with such representations. An algebraic language can remove the difficulties.

Let T represent the arena, as depicted in Figure 1.1. Images of this arena presented to X, Y, and Z will be denoted by Tx, Ty, and Tz, respectively. (Read, "T from X's position, T from Y's position," etc.) Tx, Ty, and Tz are results of "becoming aware." Now images within personae can be assimilated by other personae, generating Txy, Txz, Tyz, etc. (Read, "Tx from Y's position," etc.) Analogously, we can define Txyz, Txzy, etc. An image acquired by a persona at time t_1 can also be assimilated at time t_2, being an image of an image. We may, therefore, have Txx, Tyy, etc.

Next, we represent the interrelations of the three personae. At time t_0, we have no internal images within the personae (Figure 1.1). The system is represented by T and we shall write

$$\Omega_0 = T. \tag{0}$$

The reflexive system shown in Figure 1.2 will be represented by the sum

$$\Omega_1 = T + Tx, \tag{1}$$

where the two terms represent respectively the arena itself and the image of the arena within X.[1] The system shown in Figure 1.3 can be represented by the polynomial

$$\Omega_2 = T + Tx + (T + Tx)y.[1] \tag{2}$$

Here (T + Tx)y represents the picture in Figure 1.2 inserted inside Y in Figure 1.3. After Z has, in turn, become aware of the situation, we can easily represent the system by

$$\Omega_3 = T + Tx + (T + Tx)y + [T + Tx + (T + Tx)y] z. \tag{3}$$

Introducing a distributive law permits the removal of parentheses. For example,

$$T + Tx + (T + Tx)y = T + Tx + Ty + Txy.$$

The distributive law can be interpreted in two ways. An index taken outside a parenthesis can be viewed from the position of an outside observer. By this operation the observer exhibits the inner worlds of the different personae, which he can then examine as entire entities. This does not mean, however, that the personae have this integrated image. On the other hand, the operation can be viewed as the appearance of an integrated image within a persona.

Next, terms may be repeated without changing the meaning of a polynomial:

$$T + Tx = T + Tx + Tx.$$

That is to say, a persona (or the observer) gets no more information if a text already known to him is repeated. We have, in fact, introduced the principle of idempotency into our algebra, whereby our polynomials can be regarded as having Boolean coefficients:

$$Tx + Tx = 1 \cdot Tx + 1 \cdot Tx = (1 + 1)Tx = 1 \cdot Tx = Tx.$$

Note that the polynomials say nothing about the validity of the images in the personae. Thus Txy says only that y has an image of Tx, which may or may not correspond to Tx. Therefore, in applying the notation, it is necessary to comment on the adequacy of the images from the position of the external observer.

The Operator of Awareness

A reflexive polynomial registers the structure of the state of a system. We have seen how successive acts of awareness change this state. To find an algebraic analogue of the act of awareness, we must find the algebraic rules whereby state Ω_0 is transformed into state Ω_1, Ω_1 into state Ω_2, etc. As we shall show, these rules consist of multiplying the polynomials on the right with $(1 + x)$, $(1 + y)$, etc. Thus,

$$\Omega_1 = \Omega_0 * (1 + x) = T * (1 + x) = T + Tx$$

$$\Omega_2 = \Omega_1 * (1 + y) = (T + Tx) * (1 + y) = T + Tx + (T + Tx)y$$

$$\Omega_3 = \Omega_2 * (1 + z) = [T + Tx + (T + Tx)y] * (1 + z) =$$
$$= T + Tx + (T + Tx)y + [T + Tx + (T + Tx)y] \, z.$$

We can also write

$$\Omega_3 = T * (1 + x) * (1 + y) * (1 + z).$$

We have thus introduced two kinds of polynomials. One kind represents the states of the system; the other kind represents operators that bring the system from one state to another. Polynomials of the first kind will be denoted by Ω; of the second, by ω. We can write

$$\Omega_0 \xrightarrow{\omega} \Omega_1, \text{ or } \Omega_0 * \omega = \Omega_1.$$

As we shall show below, operators more complex than $(1 + x)$, $(1 + y)$, etc. can also be interpreted in terms of our model.
    We can also write

$$\Omega_0 * \omega_1 * \omega_2 \cdots \cdot \omega_k = \Omega_k$$

to indicate that the system passes sequentially from Ω_0 to Ω_1, $\Omega_2, \cdots \Omega_k$. Since the multiplication of reflexive polynomials is associative, we can, by shifting parentheses, arrive at another set of factors:

$$\Omega_0 * \omega_1' * \omega_2' * \cdots \cdot \omega_k = \Omega_k'$$

that is, we can find another path from Ω_0 to Ω_k.
    The product $\omega_1 * \omega_2 = \omega_{12}$ denotes a new operator of awareness, which takes the system from Ω_0 directly to Ω_2. A system can be represented either by some polynomial Ω or by a set of operators of awareness, ω_1, ω_2, $\cdots \omega_k$. Therefore, we must distinguish between the formal operation of constructing a new operator of awareness (a product of ω's) and the operation of awareness itself (applying an operator of awareness to a polynomial).
    Note two possible interpretations of the term Tx. On the one hand, we may regard it as an identification of an image assimilated by X. The element x is an index showing from

whose position the image is seen. On the other hand, x may denote X's "eye," the apparatus that characterizes X's position or even X himself. The symbol T is the image on the "retina" of this apparatus. The difference is seen more clearly when we examine the term Txy. On the one hand, xy can be regarded as markers, showing that the image T, assimilated by X, is viewed from Y's position; that is, Y reflects the representation on X's "retina." On the other hand, xy denotes the registration by Y, not only of the image reflected on X's "retina," but also the structure of X's "eye." Thus, the elements of our notation have both a marking function and a "substantive" meaning. This will become a matter of importance in Chapter 4, where the symbols T, x, y, z will acquire concrete content.

An Illustration

Consider the following passage:
"X watched a glowing sunset. Y stood nearby and also admired the sunset. Suddenly Y realized that X was deeply moved by the sight. A moment later Z came up stealthily from behind. He, too, saw the sunset. Z understood very well that X and Y were both absorbed by the sight of the setting sun and that Y was also observing the impression that this sight exerted on X. This realization was painful to Z."

The principal content of the passage can be symbolized as follows:

T   :   the sunset as seen by an outside observer.

Tx   :   X saw the setting sun.

Ty   :   Y saw the setting sun.

Txy   :   Y realized that X was impressed by the sight.

Tz   :   Z saw the setting sun.

Txz   :   Z realized that X was absorbed by the sight.

Tyz   :   Z realized that Y was absorbed by the sight.

Txyz :   Z realized that Y observed the impression that the sight made on X.

Summing the elements and rewriting, we have

$$\Omega = T + Tx + Ty + Txy + Tz + Txz + Tyz + Txyz$$

$$= T + Tx + (T + Tx)y + [T + Tx + (T + Tx)y] \ z.$$

The last expression is equivalent to (3). Inside the parentheses and brackets are the inner worlds of our personae. The notation exhibits not only the final situation but also the dynamics of its development, namely, the successive acts of awareness performed by the three personae. Clearly, the symbolism represents an abstraction from the concrete situation (the setting sun, the nature of the relationships among the personae, etc.). Only the reflexive structure of the situation in its pure form has been identified.[2]

The Formalism

Formally our algebraic system is defined in terms of the following notation and rules of operation.

1. We have a given set of symbols x, y, z, T, 1.

2. Symbols written sequentially and not separated by commas will be called *words*.

3. Two words differing only in the number of occurrences of "1" are equivalent. That is, "1" may be canceled in any word except when the word consists of a single "1."

4. Polynomials are of the form

$$\omega = \sum_{i=1}^{n} \alpha_i \ a_i$$

   where α_i are Boolean functions and a_i are words. If $a_k = a_l$, then

   $$\alpha_k a_k + \alpha_l a_l = (\alpha_k + \alpha_l)a_k.$$

5. Addition of polynomials is commutative:

   $$\omega_1 + \omega_2 = \omega_2 + \omega_1.$$

6. The product of two polynomials $\sum\limits_{i=1}^{n} \alpha_i \, a_i$ and $\sum\limits_{j=1}^{m} \beta_j \, b_j$ is defined as

$$\omega_1 * \omega_2 = \sum_{i=1}^{n} \sum_{j=1}^{m} \alpha_i \, \beta_j \, a_i b_j.$$

7. We postulate

$$\omega^0 = 1.$$

It is easy to see that multiplication is associative but in general not commutative. Also the right and left distribution laws hold:

$$(\omega_1 + \omega_2) * \omega_3 = \omega_1 * \omega_3 + \omega_2 * \omega_3;$$

$$\omega_3 * (\omega_1 + \omega_2) = \omega_3 * \omega_1 + \omega_3 * \omega_2.$$

We recall the Boolean operations to be used below:

$$1' = 0; 0' = 1; \alpha + \alpha = \alpha; \alpha^n = \alpha; \alpha \alpha' = 0; \alpha + \alpha' = 1.$$

Words not containing T will be denoted by u_i. Two classes of polynomials will be distinguished. Those of the first class, to be designated by Ω, are in the form

$$\Omega = T + \sum_{i=1}^{n} \alpha_i T u_i;$$

those of the second class, to be denoted by ω are of the form

$$\omega = \sum_{i=1}^{k} \alpha_i u_i.$$

Recall that the polynomials of the first class represent the state of a reflexive system; those of the second class operators of awareness.

Differences between our algebra and ordinary algebra can be seen in the following identities:

$$(1 + \omega)^n = 1 + \omega + \omega^2 + \cdots \omega^n$$

$$= 1 + \omega + (1 + \omega)^2 + \cdots (1 + \omega)^n;$$

$$(T + \Omega\omega) * (1 + \omega)^n = T + \Omega_n * \omega, \tag{4}$$

where $\quad \Omega_n = T * (1 + \omega)^{n-1} + \Omega * (1 + \omega)^n.$

Identity (4) will be interpreted below in a way important for this discussion. It can be derived by direct substitution for Ω_n. Note that the factorization of polynomials into "prime" factors is not unique. We have, for example,

$$1 + x + x^2 + x^3 = (1 + x)^3 = (1 + x) * (1 + x^2).$$

Formally, the multiplication operator * may be omitted:

$$(T + Tx) * y = (T + Tx)y.$$

Note, however, the different interpretations of the two expressions. The left side represents an act of awareness performed by Y with respect to the image $(T + Tx)$. The right side is the result of the operation.

Consider now the expression $T * x + Tyx$. It can be formally "factored," that is, written as $(T + Ty) * x$. Now X's position with respect to Ty is no longer expressed. But we now have Y's position with respect to T, which did not appear in the original expression. Rewritten as $(T + Ty)x$, the expression represents the external observer's position with respect to T.

In the expression $(T * x)y$, the symbol T represents the image of T, not from the position of the external observer, but from that of Y, since everything within the parentheses refers to Y's inner world. On the other hand, in the expression $(T * x) * y$, T represents the image presented to the observer. Keeping in mind the possibility of losing or gaining positions, we may perform operations regardless of whether they stand next to each other or are separated by *.

In our previous illustrations, the personae performed their respective acts of awareness sequentially. If they perform them simultaneously in successive moments of time, the system will pass through the following states:

$$\Omega_0 = T,$$

$$\Omega_1 = T + Tx + Ty + Tz,$$

$$\Omega_2 = T + (T + Tx + Ty + Tz)x + (T + Tx + Ty + Tz)y +$$

$$(T + Tx + Ty + Tz)z.$$

And in general, as is easy to see,

$$\Omega_n = T + (1 + x + y + z)^n.$$

Thus, the system is brought from one state to the next by an operator of awareness in the form

$$\omega = 1 + x + y + z.$$

Here the operator characterizes the entire system rather than a single persona. The individual personae are equipped with operators $(1 + x)$, $(1 + y)$, and $(1 + z)$ respectively. However, because they are acting together, the system is characterized by a single operator of awareness instead of by three different operators.

Closed Operators

Consider a system represented by a polynomial in the form

$$T + (\Omega + \Omega y)x. \tag{5}$$

The reality, which X sees as presented to him, is seen by him as also reflected by Y. (We assume, of course, that not only the structures but also the contents of both Ω's are identical.) Imagine that X regards himself to be in conflict with Y. Whether Y exists from the point of view of an external observer or only within X's inner world is immaterial to us. What matters is that X makes his decisions assuming that Y is an opponent and that any decision felt by X to be his own is reflected (it appears to him) by Y. Consider a decision (or a strategy) somehow dependent on the arena presented to X. Denote it by S(T), and let $\Omega = (T + Tx)$. Then (5) becomes

$$[T + (T + Tx) + (T + Tx)y] \, x.$$

We represent the dependence of S on T as follows:

Since X believes that his strategy is reflected by Y, Y becomes a sort of "all-seeing eye," able to read X's thoughts and to anticipate his strategy.[3] Given this structure, X must profess the maximin principle; that is, he must choose strategies which, if made known to Y, will enable Y to minimize X's gain, that is, strategies that will minimize X's loss.

In many conflicts, however, such "optimal" strategies do not exist. The persona (player) is forced to neutralize the opponent's deduction by randomizing his decisions, so that the opponent, even if he can read X's thoughts, cannot deduce his strategy (assuming that a randomly determined event cannot be anticipated with certainty). However, the opponent will know that X has used a random device in choosing his strategy. The classical theory of games, developed by John von Neumann, answers the question how a random device is to be used in situations of this sort.

The reflexive structure given by (5) is not, in general, constant. Suppose, for example, X is equipped with the operator $(1 + x)$ and so has become aware of his state:

$$[T + (\Omega + \Omega y)x] * (1 + x) = T + (T + \Omega + \Omega x + \Omega y + \Omega yx)x.$$

The new state is no longer representable in the form

$$T + (\Omega' + \Omega'y)x,$$

where Ω' is some appropriate polynomial. Thus, whereas prior to applying $(1 + x)$, X professed the maximin principle, he now passes into a state where it makes no sense to apply this principle, since it is no longer true that any decision, which X sees as his own, is replicated by Y. For instance, if the argument for a decision is the term Ωy, then this decision is no longer replicated by Y:

$$\text{S} \atop \uparrow$$

$$T + (T + \Omega + \Omega x + \Omega y + \boxed{\Omega y}\ x)x$$

Thus, the "maximin policy" turns out to be unsuitable if a persona is equipped with $(1 + x)$. This suggests the following question: Is there an operator of awareness which preserves the state in which an opponent appears to read any thought occurring to the persona, of which the persona is aware of as his own? Such an operator $(1 + \omega)$, must satisfy the following condition: the expression $[T + (\Omega + \Omega y)x] *$ $(1 + \omega)^n$ must be representable in the form $T + (\Omega_n + \Omega_n y)x$ for any positive integer n, where no a priori restrictions are imposed on Ω_n. If this condition is satisfied, Y remains a "majorant," that is, empowered to read any thought occurring to X. The simplest operator satisfying the above condition is

$$(1 + \omega) = 1 + x + yx.$$

This follows from the more general identity

$$(T + \Omega\omega) * (1 + \omega)^n = T + \Omega_n\omega, \tag{4}$$

where $\omega = x + yx$, as was shown on page 54. If a persona is equipped with a single operator $(1 + x + yx)$, and if his initial state is $\Omega_0 = T$, he is destined to profess the maximin principle, since he will remain "locked in" in a set of states in which Y is a majorant:

$$\Omega = T * (1 + x + yx)^n.$$

Note that this polynomial can be expanded via sequential acts of awareness without any external information input. New information results from a reflexion of a previous state. In other words, the operator that generates the maximin principle is a special form of self-awareness.

Of course, T need not be the initial state for closure to occur. Successive applications of the operator $1 + x + yx$ to any expression in the form

$$\Omega_n = T(1 + x)^n$$

will generate states in the form

$$\Omega' = T + (\Omega + \Omega y)x.$$

In fact, we have

$$T(1 + x)^n = T + \sum_{i=0}^{n} Tx^i;$$

$$(T + \sum_{i}^{n} Tx^i)(1 + x + yx) = T + \sum_{i}^{n} Tx^i + \sum_{i}^{n} Tx^{i+1} + \sum_{i}^{n} Tx^i yx$$

$$= T + \sum_{i}^{n} x^{i+1} + \sum_{i}^{n} Tx^i yx = T + (\sum_{i}^{n} Tx^i + \sum_{i}^{n} Tx^i y)x$$

$$= T + (\Omega' + \Omega'y)x.$$

Note also that the state $T + (\Omega + \Omega x)y$, which is "preserved" by the operator $1 + x + yx$ is not necessarily generated by it.

Consider the operator

$$\omega' = 1 + x + x^2 + yx + xyx.$$

It can be easily seen that this operator is not a power of $1 + x + yx$. Let the state of the system be generated by a single application of ω'. We can represent the state of the system in the form

$$\Omega = T + Tx + Tx^2 + Tyx + Txyx$$

$$= T + [(T + Tx) + (T + Tx)y]\, x = T + (\Omega' + \Omega'y)x.$$

We might conjecture that the type of operator that generates the maximin principle underlies some types of religious thinking. The God of the Calvinists is an "all-seeing eye" and controls all thought. The operator of awareness is not controlled by the persona. An act of awareness is a "natural event." These beliefs may lead to paradoxical states painful to the believer. If he thinks he is an unbeliever, this belief is "majorized" in consequence of the nature of the operator. God continues to exist in his inner world.

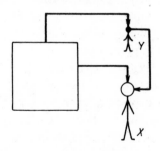

Figure 1.4

Figure 1.4 illustrates the situation. X is equipped with a screen of awareness, represented by the square. The manikin Y is attached to this screen. Although this manikin is outside the screen, he is conceived by X. The image projected on the screen enters X along two channels, directly from the screen and indirectly from Y, who cannot be removed by an act of awareness since this act originates in an image inside the screen. In particular, if a situation like the one pictured in Figure 1.4 is reflected on the screen, this does not change the awareness process (cf., Figure 1.5) just as the projection of the mechanism of a projector upon the moving picture screen has no effect on the projector. The image on the screen will still enter X along two channels.

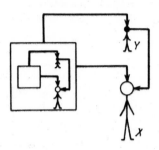

Figure 1.5

Although this graphical representation of an operator of awareness does not register the more subtle features of the process, it does register roughly some events, not captured by the algebraic apparatus. For instance, we may throw a pattern upon the screen which the persona does not distinguish from the projected image. From the position of an external observer, only a part of the total image is due to the projection, but the persona cannot separate the added elements from the projected ones.

Let us examine some other "locking in" operators, for example $(1 + x^2)$. A single application produces

$$\Omega_1 = T + Txx.$$

Assimilated by the persona is not the arena T, but rather an image of the arena reflected by himself. We are dealing here with a "solipsoidal" inner world. To X, the reality of T always appears as an element of his inner world. Awareness of Ω_1 via $(1 + x^2)$ again leads to a solipsoidal inner world, since this type of inner world is closed with respect to the given operator. In fact, we have

$$(T + \Omega x) * (1 + x^2)^n = T + \Omega_n xx.$$

The persona is destined to relate to reality only as an element of his inner world. If such a person assumes the role of an external observer, the term T does not occur in the polynomial assimilated by him. Graphically, this operator is represented by Figure 1.6.

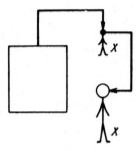

Figure 1.6

There is no direct channel from the screen of awareness to the persona. The only channel is through manikin X.

Consider now $(1 + yx)$. A single application produces

$$\Omega_1 + T + Tyx.$$

Here the world presented to X is a phenomenon within another persona. This is a pathological state, closed in virtue of the relation

$$(T + Tyx) * (1 + yx)^n = T + \Omega_n yx,$$

represented in Figure 1.7.

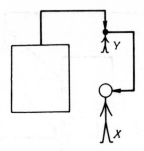

Figure 1.7

It is easy to see that the simplest operator $(1 + x)$ is likewise closed (cf., Figure 1.8).

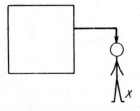

Figure 1.8

Consider now a more complex operator, which we shall need below:

$$1 + x + yx + zx + yzx.$$

Iterated applications will produce polynomials in the form

$$T + [\Omega + \Omega y + (\Omega + \Omega y)z]\, x.$$

From X's position, any image or thought perceived by him as his own is replicated by Y, while Z, who likewise replicates any thought or image which X perceives as his own, replicates the very fact that Y replicates X's thoughts or images (cf., Figure 1.9). Now we have certain personae outside the screen who are not removable by an act of awareness. These personae are in various relations of imitative subordination. We might

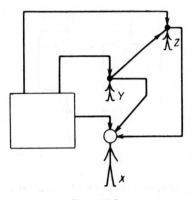

Figure 1.9

conjecture that this operator models some features of Greek Orthodox or Catholic thinking. Z is God, Y is a priest. Confession is a means of "preserving" this operator of awareness. From X's position, Y, by his actual presence, "majorizes" X's inner world. Preparing for confession and in the process of confessing, X verbalizes his inner world, expressing it in a form convenient for majorizing. Y's role is to activate the process of self-awareness, because if X is not aware of the images in his inner world, these images cannot be reflected in Z's inner world.

Different Interpretations of Operating With Reflexive Polynomials

Consider the polynomial

$$\Omega = T + Tx + Tx^2 + Tx^3 = T\,\omega = T(1 + x)^3.$$

From the position of an external observer the polynomial is naturally identified in its expanded form with the process by which it is formed. The same polynomial can be written

$$T + [T + Tx + Tx^2]\,x = T + [T(1 + x)^2]\,x.$$

Now X has been put in the position of the external observer. We can interpret this state of his inner world in two ways.

The expression on the left represents the state of the system as assimilated by him; the expression on the right represents the dynamics of formation of the state. The difference in notation can be also interpreted as a convenient way in which the external observer examines the system. The expression on the right registers only the "reduction" by the external observer of the state assimilated by X.

The personae do not perform reflexive analysis. For this reason, when we attribute to a persona an inner world represented by a polynomial, there is a danger that we make him contemplate the properties of our apparatus rather than the content that we wish to express by our symbols. In this connection, consider

$$\Omega = T + [T(1 + x)^n] \, x.$$

How shall we interpret n? If we say that n is some fixed number, the notation should be understood in the light of the comments above. Suppose, however, n is an arbitrary number from X's position. It would be senseless to say that the persona knows how the polynomial was formed, specifically, in our example, that the persona has discovered the recursive principle that generates the successive states.

Let us therefore agree on another interpretation of n. The persona may replicate some situation which, from the position of the external observer is governed by a definite law. But the law itself is not known to the persona. We can interpret the polynomial

$$\Omega = T + [T(1 + x + y)^n] \, x$$

as registering the fact that some machine is working inside X which "drives" the parameter n over the natural integers. Here the notation registers the dynamics of the process, not the identification of the principle. In the next section, where we discuss Prisoner's Dilemma, the above expression will be understood in just this way.

Reflexive Polynomials That Generate Prisoner's Dilemma

Prisoner's Dilemma is an excellent illustration of a situation where conventional conceptions of rational behavior do not apply. According to Anatol Rapoport, Prisoner's Dilemma belongs to the paradoxes which "at times appear on the intellectual horizon as harbingers of important scientific and philosophical discoveries" (Rapoport, 1965).

The dilemma arises as follows. Two suspects are arrested and isolated from each other. The prosecutor is convinced that they committed a serious crime but does not have sufficient evidence to charge them. Each prisoner is told that he has two alternatives, to confess to the crime or not. If neither confesses, they will be charged with a minor crime and both will receive a mild sentence. If both confess, both will receive a more severe sentence, but the prosecutor will not demand the maximum penalty. If only one confesses, his sentence will be greatly reduced (to less than the sentence for the minor crime), while the other, who refused to confess, will suffer the maximum penalty.

The situation is represented in the following matrix.

	Confess	Not confess
Confess	5, 5	1, 15
Not confess	15, 1	2, 2

The alternatives are represented by the rows and columns of the matrix. The first entry in each cell is the length of the prison sentence in years received by the prisoner choosing the corresponding row. The second entry is the column chooser's punishment.

Let us see how a prisoner's lawyer will advise him. X's lawyer will certainly advise X to confess, since this is the only advice that will not subsequently elicit an objection by his client. In fact, if Y does not confess, X will receive only one year; if Y does confess, the lawyer will have saved X from a fifteen-year sentence, which he would have received if he did not confess.

Y's lawyer will advise *his* client to confess for the same reasons. Thus, if both prisoners follow their lawyers' advice, both will receive five-year sentences. The lawyers can, of course, be replaced by inner voices that suggest the above prudent strategies. However, two other voices advise the prisoners not to confess. If they follow *this* advice, each will receive only a two-year sentence.

To facilitate the analysis of the reflexive structures that generate the dilemma, we shall present another example:

X and Y are armed with pistols. If X kills Y, he gets a ruble; if Y kills X, he gets a ruble. Neither a moral nor a legal stigma is attached to the killings. The "players" must make decisions independently of each other and cannot communicate. How shall each decide? X reasons as follows:

"If I shoot, I either win a ruble or I die. If I don't shoot, I certainly won't win a ruble, and I might die. The probability that I die is not diminished if I don't shoot, because my opponent makes his decision independently. However, the opponent will reason in the same way as I; so he, too, will shoot. Maybe if I don't shoot, he won't either. But, no, this doesn't follow, because our decisions aren't linked. Certainly it is to the advantage of both of us *not* to shoot. Reasoning as I do, he will deduce this; so he won't shoot. Aha! Then I shall shoot and win a ruble. But he, too, will come to the same decision. . . ."

Here a player attempting to make a decision is confronted with repeated contradictions. Neither alternative is convincing. To bring out the paradox, imagine the two separated by a mirror. X lifts his pistol and sees that the image of his "opponent" does the same and that the expression on his face is menacing. X understands that if he presses the trigger, the image will, too. X lowers the pistol. The "opponent" does the same.

"I shall now fool him," thinks X, "since he, too, must see the same sort of image." Immediately a sly expression appears on the face of the image and a preparatory movement of the pistol. . . .

X, who uses himself as a model of his opponent, can be represented by

$$\Omega_n = T + (Tx + Ty)x + (Tyx + Txy)x + (Txyx + Tyxy)x + \ldots$$

From X's position each image assimilated by himself is assimilated also by Y. It is impossible to express a process preserving the symmetric structure "inside" X by means of an external multiplier. We must introduce an "imbedded" operator of awareness. Formally, the above polynomial may be written as

$$\Omega_n = T + T(1 + x + y)^n x.$$

For any value of n, X's inner world will be represented by a symmetric polynomial.

It is important to note that although the decisions of the two opponents are mirrored in X's inner world, they are not simultaneous in the "living flow of thought."

"Aha! I shall shoot and win a ruble," relates to moment 1.

"But he will arrive at the same decision," relates to moment 2.

At moment 1 symmetry is violated, but it is restored at moment 2. It is these oscillations that generate the dilemma. They are not reflected in the notation

$$\Omega = T + [T(1 + x + y)^n]x.$$

P. V. Baranov proposed to rewrite the preceding expression as

$$= T + \left\{ T + T\left[x\left(1 + \frac{y}{x}\right)\right]^n \right\}x.$$

Although the concept of quotient was not introduced rigorously here, the meaning of the latter formula is evident. Note once again that in our model the operator of awareness works "automatically." It is not controlled by the persona's "will." The process generated by the operator consists of two phases. In the first phase, X performs the act of awareness and decides to shoot; in the second, Y makes the same decision, and X deduces that neither of them ought to shoot. Then everything is repeated. We see that in this model the player *will never shoot! But this does not mean that the dilemma has been resolved.* It is the player who does not shoot who faces the dilemma. He vacillates: Shall he shoot or not? He does not shoot because he has not made a decision, not because he has *decided* not to shoot. It is very important to distinguish these two kinds of "not shooting."

In the context of this dilemma, it is impossible to adopt an optimal decision. The paradox originates in the player who, using a particular model of his opponent, adopts what seems an optimal decision, but which turns out to be a fatal one. Note that if X were "constructed" otherwise, for instance, if he were equipped with the operator $\omega = 1 + x + yx$ which would take him into the state

$$\Omega = T + (\Omega + \Omega y)x,$$

he would not be in a dilemma. For, suppose that X decides not to shoot. Since Y is here an "all-seeing eye" who reads X's thoughts, he will decide to shoot in order to win his ruble. Therefore, only one alternative remains—to shoot.[4]

We conclude, therefore, that the dilemma is generated by a sequential violation and restoration of the symmetric structure of the player's inner world. Prisoner's Dilemma cannot be resolved, but it can be explained.

Positive and Negative Forms

Consider

$$\Omega = T + (T + Tx^3)x + (T + Tx + Tx^2 + Ty)y$$

TABLE 1

T	Tx	Tx^4	Ty	Txy	Tx^{2}y	Ty^2			Observer
T							Tx^3		X
T	Tx		Ty					Tx^2	Y

as usual representing a system from the position of an external observer. Table 1 shows the elements in the inner worlds of the personae and those seen by the external observer.

The empty cells in the first seven columns correspond to terms that are present from the position of the external observer but absent in the inner worlds of the personae. We see also that X and Y have terms that do not occur in the polynomial representing the position of the external observer, namely Tx^3 and Tx^2.

We now introduce a notation for terms "not known" to particular personae. For example, Tx is not known to X since only T and Tx^3 are contained in his inner world. We shall denote this fact by Tx$\bar{x}$ (read: "Tx is not assimilated by X"). Terms like Tx$^4\bar{x}$, Ty$\bar{x}$, etc., will have analogous meanings. Terms like Tx$^4\bar{y}$, Txy$\bar{y}$, etc. will have corresponding meaning with regard to Y.

Now we can add these terms to Ω and, applying the distributive law to x and y, we can factor them out to obtain

$$\Omega^* = T + (T + Tx^3)x + (T + Tx + Tx^2 + Ty)y + (Tx +$$

$$Tx^4 + Ty + Txy + Tx^2y + Ty^2)\bar{x} + (Tx^4 + Txy + Tx^2y + Ty^2)\bar{y}.$$

Clearly, every finite polynomial Ω can be represented in the form

$$\Omega^* = T + \Omega^1 x + \Omega^2 y + \Omega^3\bar{x} + \Omega^4\bar{y}.$$

This notation enables us to register not only the contents of the inner worlds, but also terms that do not occur there but do occur in the system from the position of an external observer.

Terms of Ω^* contained in Ω will be called a *positive form*, the sum $\Omega^3 \bar{x} + \Omega^4 \bar{y}$, correspondingly, a *negative form*.

The Reflexive Polynomial as a Means of Registering Constraints

Imagine that every inhabitant of a city, sitting in the evening in front of his fireplace, has become independently and absolutely convinced that the performance to be given on the following day by a visiting circus has been canceled. Next, the radio announces that the performance has indeed been canceled. We ask whether as a consequence of this announcement each inhabitant has received new information. At first thought, it seems that he has not, since he already knew the content of the message. As a matter of fact, however, he has received new information, since, in consequence of the announcement, he now knows that everyone else knows that the performance has been canceled (which he did not know before).

Denote the inhabitants by e_1, e_2, $\cdots$ e_k. We represent an inhabitant's becoming convinced that the performance has been canceled by

$$T + Te_i.$$

Other inhabitants together with their inner worlds do not occur in e_i's inner world.

Using the negative form, the situation from the position of the external observer can be represented by

$$\Omega^* = T + Te_i + \sum_j Te_j\bar{e}_i.$$

The broadcast removes the bar over e_i, transforming Ω^* into

$$\Omega^{**} = T + Te_i + \sum_j Te_je_i = T + (T + \sum_j Te_j)e_i.$$

We see, therefore, that making public a piece of information already known to everyone produces changes in the reflexive polynomial: It now contains the inner worlds of other personae with information received by them.

Reflexive analysis does not enable us to examine the process of decision-making as such. It only sets a framework that identifies the "type of information" that may be involved in the generation of decisions.

When we consider each inhabitant before he has heard the radio announcement, we have to take into account only one constraint, namely the absence of Te_j terms in his inner world: He himself "knows" but does not realize that the others may also "know." The radio announcement carries the persona into another state. The terms Te_j have appeared in his inner world, but the terms Te_je_k are still missing. The constraints have changed.

Let X be represented by

$$\Omega = T + (T + Tx)x.$$

Using the positive-negative form, we can rewrite the expression as

$$\Omega^* = T + (T + Tx)x + Txx\bar{x}.$$

The term $Txx\bar{x}$, registering the fact that Txx is "unknown" to the persona (but is known to the external observer), shows that the persona cannot utilize that term in a conscious formulation of a decision. The persona is "free" only within the bounds of his inner world, represented by $(T + Tx)$.

Suppose now the persona has performed the act of awareness by means of the operator $(1 + x)$:

$$[T + (T + Tx)x] (1 + x) = T + (T + Tx + Txx)x.$$

Now the restriction has been removed: Txx is known to X. However, he still does not know Txxx. He is freer than before, but still restricted.

In this context, let us examine the locking-in operators. As has been shown, these operators, while changing polynomials, leave certain of their properties invariant. This invariance can be viewed as a restriction of a higher order, as it were. A locking-in operator fails to remove certain *structural* restrictions. A persona equipped with just one locking-in operator remains "locked in" in a class of polynomials having a particular structure. Only a change of operator "frees" him, allows him to escape from that class of polynomials. In this sense, any function defined on a set of reflexive polynomials and deriving meaning from the same set can be regarded as a particular operator of awareness. To be sure, we shall extend the phrase "becoming aware" to transformations involving the simplification of polynomials. In this case, restrictions are strengthened rather than weakened, and the persona loses rather than gains freedom.

Chapter 2

FOCAL POINTS

Imagine a Prisoner in a cell shown in Figure 2.1.

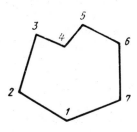

Figure 2.1

Outside is his friend who wants to free him. Neither can pierce the wall alone, but if they drill from opposite sides in the same spot, they can do it. Suppose it is possible to pierce the wall only at points 1, 2, ... 7. Communication between them being impossible, neither knows which point the other will choose. How shall "rational" partners behave? It is intuitively clear and can be shown experimentally that 4 will be chosen. How can the two minds converge without communication? Convergence at 4 is not accidental if the two reflexive systems interact by replicating each other.

It is clear to us (since we ourselves are reflexive systems) that corner 4 should be chosen, because it is "peculiar."[5] But why should there be a leaning toward the "peculiar?" Problems of this sort, related to convergence without preliminary agreement, were discussed by T. Schelling (1960).

Schelling called such "peculiar" features *focal points* and gave several interesting examples without, however, clarifying the logico-psychological mechanism of the phenomenon. It would seem that a reflexive chain in the form of "I think that he thinks that I think . . ." could serve as an explanation of how focal points function. However, the method explains only those cases where a preference among outcomes is given. For example, if two people try to meet in a park when it is raining, and if there is a pavillion in the park, the chain of reasoning will lead to a solution via the chain, "I think that he thinks that I think that the pavillion is protection against the rain." But the explanation does not apply to our example with the prison. The "special" corner has no objective advantage (nor a subjective one like tradition). For this reason, the chain, "I think that he thinks . . ." cannot be closed by a rational choice. In our opinion, reflexive analysis can explain the appearance of focal points because it can operate with structures more complex than "I think that he thinks that I think . . ."

Structures in the form "I think that he thinks . . ." are represented by reflexive polynomials in the form

$$T + \left\{ T + [(T + Ty)]\, x \right\} y.$$

X is in Y's inner world, and Y is in X's. The imbedding can be of arbitrary depth. For such simple structures an abbreviated representation can be used. For instance, the above polynomial can be replaced by the expression $\overrightarrow{YXY}$ (read, "Y thinks that X thinks that Y thinks") and similarly for longer chains.

Note that such structures fall into two classes, those with an odd, and those with an even number of factors. The *rank of reflexion* of a persona can be introduced to characterize the "depth of simulation" represented by the number of successive imbeddings of other personae by the persona in question (Lefebvre, 1965a).

Let us now consider the operator of awareness $(1 + x + yx)$ and the polynomial generated by it,

$$\Omega = T + (\Omega + \Omega y)x.$$

We have seen that in a conflict situation this operator generates the maximin strategy. In Prisoner's Dilemma, exemplified by the pistol shooters, it generates a shot. Let now the Prisoner in Figure 2.1 be equipped with this operator. From his position, his partner replicates his every thought. Let us distinguish between a decision and the realization of a decision. The former is an element of the persona's inner world; the latter a component of his behavior. Reasoning supports the choice of an alternative; it does not completely determine the choice. Reasoning based on repeatedly encountered features of a situation will yield a multiple-valued decision. Reasoning based on an exclusive feature will yield a single-valued decision. If, for instance, six corners are red and one is green, the decision to choose red implies six equi-valued variants. If the prisoner feels that his thought is simulated by his partner, then the advantage lies with the decision with the smallest number of variants.

The difference between the way the operator $\omega = 1 + x + yx$ works in the context of a conflict and in the context of pursuit of a common goal by two players can be explained as follows. Let X attempt to avoid contact with Y while Y tries to contact X. Let X have a choice among a set of white and black sites where he can hide. We suppose that X can distinguish only white from black, not the positions of the sites or any other feature. Hence he has just two choices available, "white" and "black." Let white sites be more numerous than black sites. Since from his position the opponent can replicate any thought of his, X should choose a white site in order to minimize the probability that the opponent will find him. Note that the general idea to hide in an otherwise un-labeled element belonging to the larger subset is apparently determined by the operator $\omega = 1 + x + yx$. If X were repre-sented by a polynomial in the form

$$\Omega = T + [T + T(1 + x + yx)^n y] \, x,$$

where n is an arbitrary integer, then whatever decision X arrives at must appear wrong as soon as the operator ω is applied; since when this occurs, X becomes aware that Y has replicated his decision. As pointed out above, repeated application of ω generates the maximin principle. Let θ be the fraction of white sites and $1 - \theta$ the fraction of black sites, where $\theta > 1 - \theta$ (cf., Figure 2.2). We can associate X's payoffs with the probability that X escapes from Y. Then these payoffs will be represented by θ and $1 - \theta$, *regardless* of whether X hides in a white or a black site. We conclude that in the given conflict situation, X will be indifferent between the decision to hide in a white or a black site.

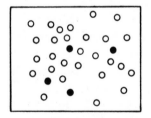

Figure 2.2

Now consider the case where X and Y are trying to meet in one of the sites represented in Figure 2.2. X, who is en-dowed with a single operator,

$$\omega = 1 + x + yx,$$

will choose a black site in view of the above argument, since he is now trying to *maximize* the probability that Y will find him.

In this way, when the two are trying to solve a common problem and are unable to communicate, application of the operator $\omega = 1 + x + yx$ generates the phenomenon of a focal point. (In our case, we have a "focal set," since all black sites are indistinguishable.) If Y is "constructed" in the same way, that is, has his own operator $\omega = 1 + y + xy$, both will arrive at the same focal set. If this set consisted of only one site, they would meet with certainty.

Note the curious circumstance that each persona has an inadequate idea about his partner. (In reality, they are as they appear to the external investigator.)

Focal points and focal sets can be generated by operators other than $\omega = 1 + x + yx$. Consider a persona represented in the form

$$\Omega = T + [T(1 + x + y)^n] \, x.$$

We have considered this polynomial in connection with Prisoner's Dilemma. An inner world constructed in this way can also generate a focal point.

Since X's partner is identical to him, X's choice will automatically be replicated by Y. If X must choose one of the sites in Figure 2.2, he will choose a black site, since from the very fact that he so chooses, his "mirror partner" will also choose a black site.

Thus, we conclude that the phenomenon of the focal point is generated by specific reflexive structures.

It is easy to construct a situation where a persona on the one hand "generates" a focal point and on the other hand is forced to neutralize the deduction. Suppose that under the conditions of the game where the prisoner and his partner are piercing the wall from opposite sides, a third persona appears, namely Z, a guard, who intends to set a trap at one of the corners. Let the prisoner and his partner be aware of the possibility that a trap may be set. Consider X. To meet his partner, he must choose a focal point. But from his position, this choice is immediately deduced by the guard. Thus a countervailing striving appears to leave the focal point. However, the possibility of meeting the accomplice is thereby lost. We have a peculiar "fugitive's dilemma" generated by the operator $\omega = 1 + x + yx + zx + yzx$ examined above. This operator generates polynomials in the form

$$T + [\Omega + \Omega y + (\Omega + \Omega y)z] \, x.$$

The terms $\Omega + \Omega y$ generate the focal point, while the terms $(\Omega + \Omega y)z$ force the persona to neutralize the opponent's deduction.

We see that reflexive systems are endowed with a reservoir of self-organization, not present in other types of systems. It is possible for reflexive systems to function in a purposeful way even when they have no contact with each other.

Of special interest is the functioning of a system in which the information flowing among the elements is accessible to another player. This player is interested in having the elements exchange information. On the one hand, this gives him the opportunity to penetrate into the plans of the other side; on the other hand, this enables him to separate the elements hostile to him from neutral ones. He may even encourage the creation of coalitions of elements opposed to him in order to make the opponent visible. But this player is helpless if the opposing elements do not exchange information, utilizing instead the reservoir of self-organization available to reflexive systems for carrying out synchronized opposition. In this case, the opposing player has neither information nor a visible opponent.

Although no preliminary convention is required for carrying out coordinated actions, the region of "features" must be common to all the elements. Otherwise, the elements may generate different focal points (Bongard, 1970).

The situation with the prison cell probably resembles that

in which cosmic civilizations who have no contact with each other find themselves. When we search for cosmic neighbors on the 21 cm wave length, we arrive at one such focal point. We assume that they have long guessed that we will be looking for them on this wave length. They play the part of a "majorant."

We may suppose that reflexive processes are a universal mechanism which permits cosmic civilizations to find each other or to carry out other coordinated actions with informational contact.

Appendix

Different psychological experiments could be based on the idea of focal points. We investigated the hierarchical structures of small groups using the special "field with focal points," and these focal points had different "prestige status." The subjects' task was to distribute themselves on this field without direct informational contact.*

Every group has an informal structure and a formal one. Sometimes, the official leader of such a group is not a functional leader. In such cases, there can be conflicts between the official leader and the functional leader who really makes the decisions. Also within the group, smaller alliances may appear and become antagonistic to one another. Sometimes this antagonism is latent, but it always disturbs the effective functioning of the entire group.

This investigation was begun in Moscow in 1972. The experiments were conducted using several formal groups of Russian scholars. Although the work was not completed, it gave interesting information about the potential of this method.

The basic idea of the method consists in showing to a group of subjects an electric circuit with lamps and switches turned off. The number of switches varies with the number of members in the groups. Each subject may turn on any one switch, but he cannot have contact with any of the other members of his group. He also does not know which switch they choose. All of the subjects choose a switch at the same time.**

The group is given the task of switching on all of the lights. If they are unable to do this the first time, the task will be repeated until the problem is solved. The results of each subject's attempt are shown to the members of the group.

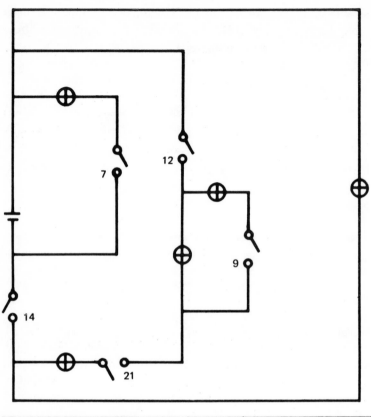

Ss	Step	1	2	3	4	5	6	7
IV	SH.	21	21	12	12	12	9	9
V	ST.	21	21	12	12	12	9	12
II	SV.	14	21	21	21	21	21	21
I	SK.	14	14	14	14	14	14	14
III	SE.	7	7	7	7	7	7	7

Figure A

We did not have the facilities to create a special experimental machine, so we drew the electric circuit on the blackboard, and subjects sitting at separate desks wrote down their particular choice of switch. After every attempt, one of the experimenters wrote down on the blackboard the number of chosen switches. The list with the names of the subjects had to be randomized. The order of the names could not be the same as the formal hierarchy. On some occasions, the experiment was set up as a competition between the two groups, and the same circuit was shown to two groups simultaneously. The task of each group was to switch on all the lights as quickly as possible (having the fewest number of attempts).

In the first circuit (Figure A), the switches have randomized numbers. The most important in this circuit is switch no. 14. The switches no. 21 and no. 12 are on the next level of importance. (The lights which were at this level would be on if switch no. 14 was already on.) The position of switch no. 21 makes it psychologically more preferable to the subjects, because it is nearer to the main switch. Switch no. 9 is destined for the "outsider" of the group—it controls only one light, and the other branches of the circuit do not depend on it. Switch no. 7 is special because its circuit is completely isolated; it does not depend on anything, and it does not influence anything. We called it the "circuit of the isolated." Using this method, we could discover some latent mutual relationships in several groups.

We were not able to complete our investigations. For this reason, we considered it expedient to describe the details of this method using a hypothetical group with an assumed formal and informal hierarchy. This gave us the possibility of explaining the peculiarities we had observed in different real groups.

Suppose the hypothetical group has five members. In Figure A their randomized list is shown. On the left, the formal status of each member of the group is indicated by roman numerals: "I" means the leader, "II" the assistant leader, etc. The columns of the table correspond to the number of attempts in the experiment. The items in the columns are the numbers of the chosen switches.

After the first attempt, let us say that only three switches were found on. The main switch, no. 14, was chosen by both subject K. and subject V. E. was the isolated subject. After the information about the options was written down in column 1, the subjects made a second attempt. V. yielded switch no. 14 to his chief. We almost always observed this effect. When a subordinate subject chose the same switch

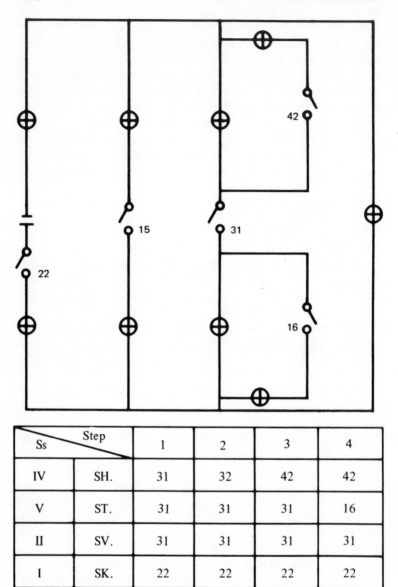

Ss \ Step	Step	1	2	3	4
IV	SH.	31	32	42	42
V	ST.	31	31	31	16
II	SV.	31	31	31	31
I	SK.	22	22	22	22
III	SE.	15	15	15	15

Figure B

as his chief, he would yield the switch on his next attempt. After the second attempt, only three switches turned on, and three members of the group claimed switch no. 21.

On the third attempt, let subject V. stay with no. 21, and two members of the group, C. and T., switch on no. 12, and continue doing so in the fourth and fifth attempts. In reality, there would be a fight for a place in the hierarchy with nobody wanting to yield. Let us assume that in the sixth attempt they would simultaneously decide to yield to one another and switch on no. 9. (This observed "stubbornness" and then the simultaneous yielding were seen many times.) As no. 12 would remain off, so also would the corresponding lights. Finally, on the seventh attempt, subject H. would stay on the switch of the outsider (though his official status was higher), and subject T. would switch on no. 12. The common task of the group would be realized.

Let us suppose that, after the solution of the first task, circuit 2 (Figure B) was shown to the same team. In the first attempt subject K. would switch on no. 22, connecting the whole system with the battery, and subject E. switch no. 15, apparently intending to be independent. The rest of the members of the group would choose switch no. 31 second in importance. In the second attempt subject H. would change to switch no. 42, but the stubborn T. would stay to fight with "subject V. himself." In the third attempt the situation would not change. Only in the fourth attempt would T. switch on the suitable no. 16. The dynamic of the solution of this task reflects the fact observed many times: The intragroup fight for the place in the hierarchy obscured for the members of the group the purpose for which the group had been created.

Let us say then that circuit 3 was shown to the subjects. It is more difficult than the previous ones. Besides the usual switches there is one two-way switch, which can connect to point 19 or 91. Which side of the circuit (right or left) gets the energy depends on the location of the two-way switch. If any two members of the group choose both points 19 and 91, the two-way switch will not connect any point.

The results of the experiment with circuit 3 are shown in Figure C. For the sake of convenience we marked the switches on the left side with − (minus) and on the right with + (plus).

After the first attempt, let us say there was the following situation. Subjects K. and E. chose different points of the two-way switch so it stayed neutral, and the system did not have any electric energy. K. chose the right side and E. the left. Subjects V. and H. turned on the left switches, and T. the right one.

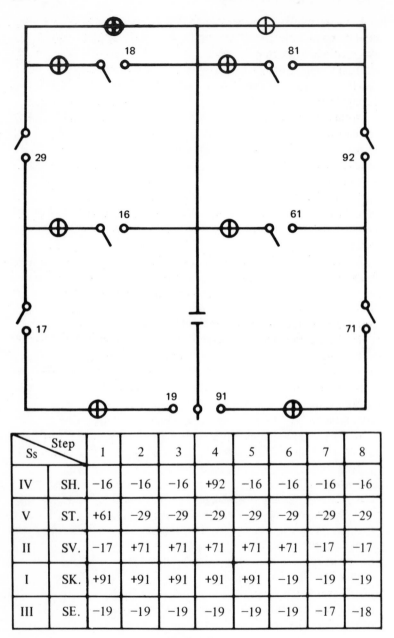

Ss	Step	1	2	3	4	5	6	7	8
IV	SH.	−16	−16	−16	+92	−16	−16	−16	−16
V	ST.	+61	−29	−29	−29	−29	−29	−29	−29
II	SV.	−17	+71	+71	+71	+71	+71	−17	−17
I	SK.	+91	+91	+91	+91	+91	−19	−19	−19
III	SE.	−19	−19	−19	−19	−19	−19	−17	−18

Figure C

In the second attempt we assume that E. would continue to choose the left point instead of "yielding to the will of the chief." K. would also continue to choose the right side whereas V. would "jump" to his chief and choose switch no. 71 on the right side of the circuit. T. would decide to support E. and choose switch no. 29 on the left side. So, during the second attempt only V. would follow K.

Nothing would change in the third attempt. K. and E. would continue their latent fight for leadership. Only V. would support K.

Suppose that in the fourth attempt H. would shift to the side of the official leader, subject K., but in the fifth attempt change his choice and shift to the side of E.

The sixth attempt would culminate in this little drama: K. would yield to E. and choose switch no. 19. Now both of them would choose one and the same switch. V. would remain the only one on the right side of the circuit.

During the seventh attempt, E. would demonstrate his tactical flexibility. He would not try for the main left switch no. 19, but yield it to his chief as a consolation gift and switch on no. 17. "Betrayed" by his chief, V. would not want to lose his place in hierarchy and choose switch no. 17, the same that was chosen by E.

In the eighth attempt E. would demonstrate that he did not want to fight with V. for the place in the hierarchy and choose the less important free switch, no. 18. His choice would completely negate the importance of this kind of hierarchy.

So, in this part of the experiment we discover that subject E. is not the "isolated" but the latent leader. He does not worry about his place in the formal hierarchy but bends his chief and the whole group to his own will, forcing them to choose the left side of the circuit.

We can assume there are two coalitions in this group: the first one between subjects K. and V., the second between E. and T. (remember that in the first attempt on circuit 3, T. chose the switch on the right side; though the formal leader opted for the right side, T. later sided with E.). It seems that H. does not participate in any stable coalition, sometimes tossed between them joining the most powerful.

Let us see the behavior of this group during the solving of task 4 (Figure D). This circuit differs from the previous one in the location of the two-way switch that commands which side of the circuit will be working. The formal leader tries to stay near the battery (the source of energy). The real leader chooses a position that permits him the maximum of option with different variations.

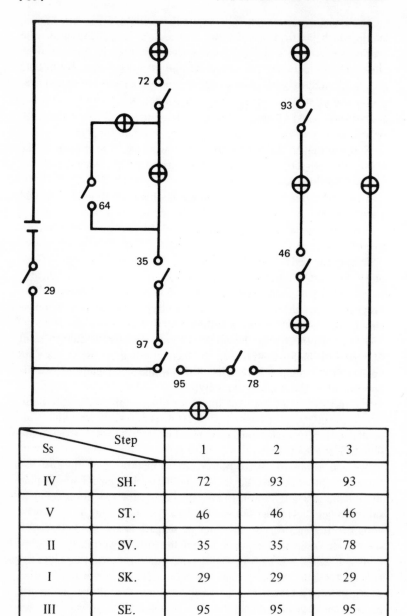

Ss	Step	1	2	3
IV	SH.	72	93	93
V	ST.	46	46	46
II	SV.	35	35	78
I	SK.	29	29	29
III	SE.	95	95	95

Figure D

The real experiment with the formal team of highly qualified scholars, in which the formal leader was also the real leader, shows that the "main" switch fell to the technical worker, and that the leader at once chose the two-way switch controlling the various options. We assume that a formal leader who is an administrator will choose the switch near the source of energy, and that a formal leader who really controls the performance of the group will choose the switch controlling the alternatives.

It is interesting that sometimes there is the phenomenon of "insurance." In some groups there are members who do not try to assume "high status" in the hierarchy, but who duplicate the choice of the more important switches and thus increasing the reliability of the group's work.

We have expounded the basic idea. In our opinion this idea may be developed and used as the basis for future concrete methods, permitting investigation of different kinds of mutual relationships among members of formal or informal group.

One of the most important characteristics of the group (within the framework of our investigation) is the speed with which they solve this kind of task (measured by the number of attempts) and their ability to transfer their experience of distribution of the switches from one task— or one set of tasks—to another.

In addition, this method can be used as a special "psychotherapeutic relaxer" of latent conflicts in real groups. The members of a group can see for themselves what kind of conflict disturbs their work and remove it with the help of the psychologist.

The set-up of the circuit task may be different from the ones described. We may use circuits in which some of the switches need to be turned off instead of on. That adds a new flavor to the "game." We may also use circuits in which the number of switches is not equal to the number of members of the group. For example, if the number of members is greater than that of switches, we may encounter "hierarchical parasitism"—when outsiders try to place themselves together with leaders. We may use a more difficult circuit with transistors and vacuum tubes with the possibility of controlling grids and capacitors, but this would be realistic only for subjects with a technical knowledge.

In the experiment with a random group of people, their distribution on switches depended on diverse factors: the order of names on the list on the blackboard, the order of switches, and most often the position of the subjects in the auditorium. Incidentally, we observed that this

"game" was usually well-accepted by the subjects. No special induce-
ment was needed to obtain the cooperation of our Soviet subjects.
Our hope is that this method may be used for comparative ethnological
investigation of different groups within modern industrial societies.

NOTES

 * This investigation was done in cooperation with Victorina Lefebvre.
 ** Another kind of experiment, but also with electric circuits with lamps and
switches, was made by Anatol Rapoport (1962). He explored the process of self-
organization. The positions of the three players were strictly predetermined in his
experiment.

Chapter 3

THE SUBCONSCIOUS

AND COMPULSION NEUROSES

So far, we have been dealing with polynomials with unit coefficients. In this chapter we consider the opportunities offered by the use of polynomials with Boolean functions as coefficients (Lefebvre, 1977).

The Representation of the Subconscious
in Reflexive Analysis

The author is obliged to apologize for a vulgarized and overly simplified treatment of the psychoanalytic view. Essentially, we shall make use of only one type of "facts": there are situations when some image A is actualized in the awareness of a subject X, which precludes the actualization of some other image B and conversely. For instance, if A is an image of the subject's own sexual life, and B is an image of his mother's sexual life, the two images (as we suppose) cannot be simultaneously actualized in X's inner world. That is, if X "sees" his own sexual life, then at that moment he cannot "see" his mother's, even though the latter is potentially present in his inner world. We shall say that the latter image exists but is not actualized when his own sexual life is actualized. If, on the other hand, the image of his mother's sexual life forms in the subject's vision, then, as if a switch occurred in a relay, his own sexual life vanishes from his "field of vision," although it remains in an unactualized form. The example is, of course, only illustrative without pretense to psychological validity.

An operator that generates the above situation is

$$\omega = 1 + \alpha x + \alpha' y, \tag{6}$$

where α and α' are Boolean functions.

Consider the polynomial

$$\Omega = T + [T(1 + \alpha x + \alpha' y)^k] \, x. \tag{7}$$

Let Y be the mother of X. Supposing $k = 1$, we obtain

$$\Omega_1 = T + [T + \alpha \, Tx + \alpha' Ty] \, x. \tag{8}$$

We shall say that an element is actualized in X's consciousness if the value of the coefficient preceding it is 1. If this value is 0, the element exists in the inner world of X in a non-actualized form. Thus, if $\alpha = 1$, $\alpha' = 0$, his own sexual life is presented to X; if $\alpha = 0$, $\alpha' = 1$, his mother's sexual life is presented while his own remains nonactualized.

The model implies the existence of certain elements that cannot be actualized in the inner world of this persona.

Suppose the operator (6) has been applied twice ($k = 2$). Then (7) becomes

$$\Omega_2 = T + [T(1 + \alpha x + \alpha' y)^2] \, x$$

$$= T + [T + \alpha \, (T + Tx)x + \alpha'(T + Ty)y + \alpha \alpha'(Txy + Tyx)] \, x.$$

The expression contains a new element. In the above polynomial,

a) $(T + Tx)x$ is an image of X's own sexual life, of which he has become aware. It is actualized when $\alpha = 1$.

b) $\alpha'(T + Ty)y$ is an image of his mother's sexual life, of which she has become aware. It is actualized when $\alpha' = 1$. But then, $\alpha = 0$, and so $(T + Tx)x$ remains nonactualized.

c) In $\alpha\alpha'(Txy + Tyx)$, Txy is X's sexual life in the eyes of his mother, and Tyx is his mother's sexual life in X's eyes. These terms denote mutual "peeking," that is, a penetration by the son into the mother's sexual life and vice versa. Since the coefficient of both terms, namely, $\alpha\alpha'$ is 0,[6] it follows that these terms can never be actualized in his inner world. Iterated applications of the operator leave the structure of the polynomial invariant. Hence his own sexual life can be repeatedly reflected and actualized by X; also his mother's sexual life can be repeatedly reflected and actualized (from X's position). But any interrelation between the two cannot be actualized.

In fact, for any k, (7) can be represented by

$$\Omega_k = T + [T + \alpha \sum_{i=1}^{k} Tx^i + \alpha' \sum_{i=1}^{k} Ty^i + \alpha\alpha' \sum_{j} Ta_j] x \qquad (9)$$

where a_j are words containing both x and y, such as xy, yx, xyx, yxy, etc. It is easy to see that only the coefficients of the "pure" powers of x and y can be different from zero. All the words Ta_j vanish identically.

Representation of "Compulsions"

Psychiatrists and neuropathologists are well acquainted with the condition wherein a patient cannot rid himself of some idea. The patient knows that it is senseless to concentrate on this idea, but he is powerless to remove it from his consciousness. A simplified model of this neurosis can be constructed by means of the operator

$$\omega = 1 + \alpha x + \alpha'x^2. \tag{10}$$

A single application yields

$$\Omega_1 = T(1 + \alpha x + \alpha'x^2) = T + (\alpha T + \alpha'Tx)x. \tag{11}$$

The persona is presented with either T or with "T from X's position." Both cannot be actualized simultaneously. If the operator is applied twice, we get

$$\Omega_2 = (T + \alpha Tx + \alpha'Tx^2)(1 + \alpha x + \alpha'x^2)$$
$$= T + [\alpha T + (\alpha + \alpha')Tx + \alpha\alpha'Tx^2 + \alpha'Tx^3]x. \tag{12}$$

In X's inner world, the elements αT and $\alpha'Tx^3$ can each be actualized. The element $\alpha\alpha'Tx^2$ has been submerged into the subconscious, whereas $(\alpha + \alpha')Tx$ is *always* actualized, since $(\alpha + \alpha') = 1$.

The persona is continually thinking about the fact that he is thinking about T, which we may interpret as a form of compulsion.

Chapter 4

SYMBOLS OF EMOTION IN

MATHEMATICAL STRUCTURES

Contemporary mathematics is not well equipped to represent the inner world of man. So far, the content of this world is more successfully reflected by artists and writers. But the language of art, being deprived of uniqueness of meanings, can be utilized in scientific work only to a limited extent. In European culture, artistic creation is specifically directed against uniqueness of meaning and against stereotypes. While some "external" structure of the inner world can be reflected in mathematical language (as in reflexive polynomials), the content of the elements which give "life" to this structure cannot be so reflected. A special system of signs is needed that would enable us to present the inner world directly. Here we shall describe a possible method of solving this problem in the framework of reflexive polynomials.

Cartoon Faces in Polynomials

Algebraic language enables us to represent the states of reflexive systems, their structures, and their potentialities for change. But the symbol Tx is faceless. It derives both its strength and its weakness from this facelessness. Its strength is in the possibility of finding a most abstract and universal means of representation. Tx can be an image visible from the position of a citizen or of a military staff or even of an entire culture. Its weakness is in the inability to reflect the specifics of the image. What the real persona sees, after all, is not T. He faces a reality, sometimes hostile, sometimes neutral, sometimes radiant. How can the content be represented in a generalized way so that at the same time the fine distinctions and nuances will also be represented?

We will depart from the mathematical tradition and will make our symbols picture the content presented to a persona. To retain its universality, the sign must not have objective content. It must express an attitude of a persona being studied toward other personae. How can such attitudes be represented? We propose to assign this task to cartoon faces.

Figure 4.1

Face 1 in Figure 4.1 is meant to represent directed fear; 2, dull acquiescence; 3, femininity; 4, gullibility; 5, indifferent intellectuality. I am sure that almost anyone can express some shades of joy or displeasure with these simple means.[7]

To be sure, there is a difficulty. Cartoon faces are mostly used as funny drawings and so carry a connotation of something flippant. I am sure, however, that their systematic use in another context will remove this connotation. And anyhow, it is not so strong as to preclude the representation of a great many expressions.

We intend to use the cartoon face as a "little gestalt" in our calculations. It is the smallest meaning-carrying unit. We need not answer the question what a face expresses. It expresses what it expresses. Translation into ordinary language is unnecessary and, at times, impossible. We cannot remain indifferent toward a cartoon face just as we cannot perceive words in our native language as simply physical sounds. Their meaning is irremovable. Cartoon faces somehow remind us of melodies. They are both meaningful and untranslatable into another language. By means of a cartoon face, the investigator can express his attitude toward any given persona. The face need not represent an individual. It is used only for its expressiveness. The referent may be a civilization or nature or a social institution. The investigator cannot be blamed for having pictured a persona by a particular face. The face serves to represent the emotional contact of a given investigator with the persona studied by him. Similarly, in modern philosophy of physics, the concept of apparatus is indispensable. The physicist relates quantum phenomena registered by a given technique not directly to the object as such, but to the object-apparatus system.

Our situation is more complex. The result is related not to some apparatus in general, but necessarily to a specific apparatus, that is to say, a particular investigator equipped with a distinct psyche. Psychological reality is many-faced. As one investigator is replaced by another, it changes. When we pass from one culture to another, catastrophical changes can occur: Entire regions of psychological reality may disappear.

In what follows, content-expressing faces will replace the symbols T, x, y, and z. For instance, the polynomial T + [T + Tx + Ty + Txy] z will be pictured as in Figure 4.2. (The "expressions" were selected arbitrarily.)

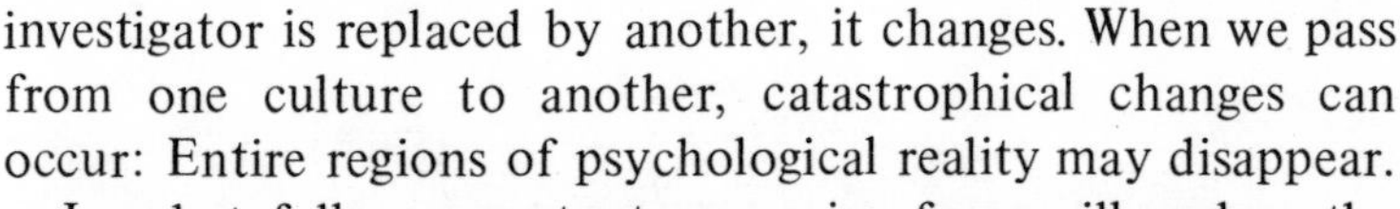

Figure 4.2

In applications, the facial expressions will be determined by the particular investigator. Reality will be represented by a square face. Its "expression" will represent the tonality of the world as presented to a particular persona. Whenever another persona's "facial expression" rather than reality is important to a persona, we shall not use a square face.

Operators of Awareness
Applied to Faces

Essentially, the notation will be the same as the algebraic except for a slight simplification: The operator $(1 + x)$ will be replaced by a single face, x. The act of awareness will be represented in Figure 4.3.

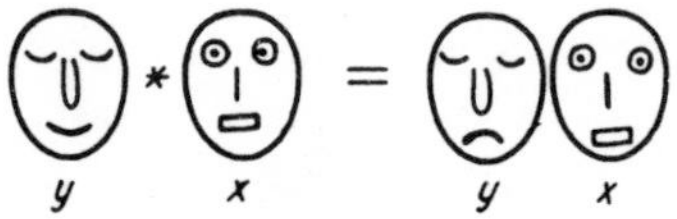

Figure 4.3

On the left, X and Y are shown from the position of an external observer; on the right, Y is an element in X's inner world.

A persona who performs an act of awareness may entertain certain stereotypes; see, for instance, Figure 4.4.

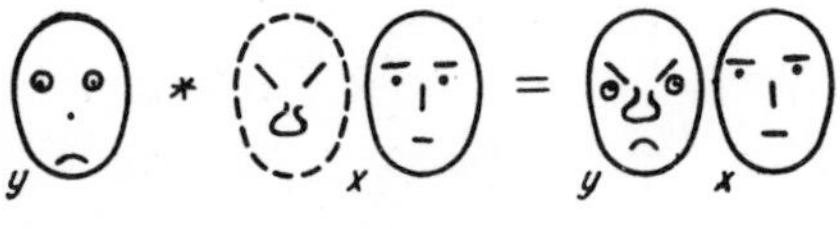

Figure 4.4

Here X's inner image contains some "a priori" features, such as a nose and eyebrows. These are invariant in his awareness. It is in this framework that Y is reflected. Any persona reflected by X will acquire that kind of nose and eyebrows. This does not exhaust all the possibilities. Figure 4.5 represents a situation where X has a *standard image of himself* in

Figure 4.5

the eyes of others. This is a peculiarity of his operator of awareness, independent of the persona reflected. In the above example, Y has no internal images. However, an act of awareness performed by X gives Y a standard image of X (from X's position).

Faces in Equations

Suppose that in the course of some experiment we obtain the data in Figure 4.6.

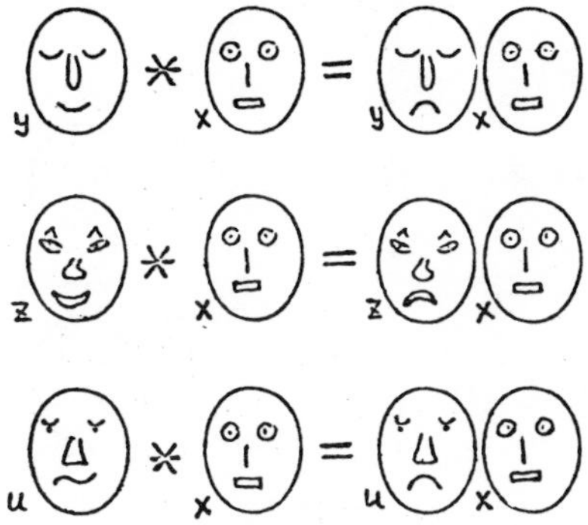

Figure 4.6

X reflects Y, Z, and U. On the left, they are represented from the position of an external observer; in the third column, from X's position. We want to know how another persona V will look from X's position (cf., Figure 4.7).

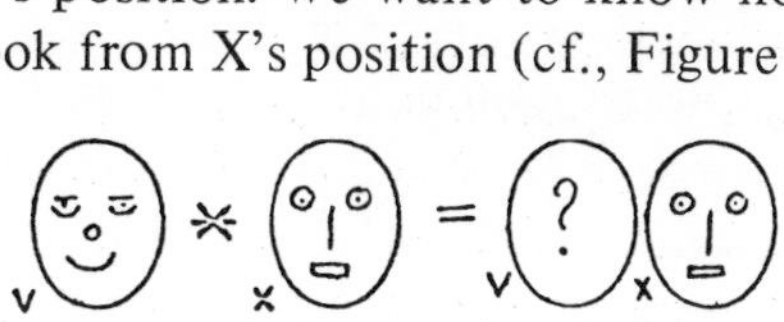

Figure 4.7

We have no data related to V; but we have data that enable us to analyze a systematic transformation performed by X. In this way, we have the possibility of discovering certain individual peculiarities of X's reflexive analysis. This example reminds us of certain formulations by H. J. Eysenck, where the subject "mobilizes his induction," that is, he is obliged to discover and to continue some regularity. In our case, we have discovered that X lowers the corners of the mouth in his images. But there are cases where a nuance must be continued that cannot be clearly defined (cf., Figure 4.8).

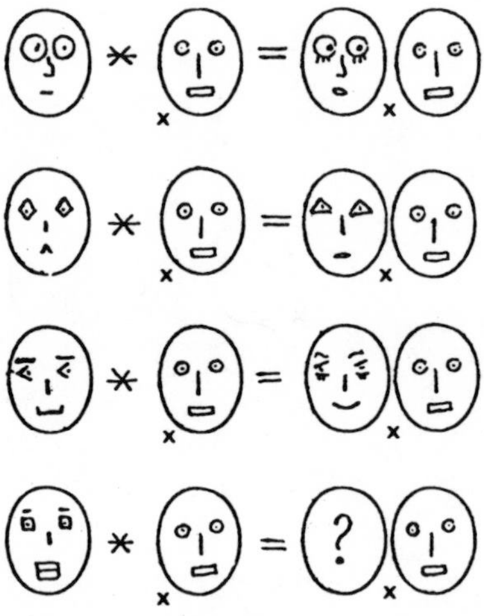

Figure 4.8

Here X transforms the reflected personae by making them somewhat "feminine" while retaining the main structural features of the drawing.

The fact that a small drawing made by a few strokes of a pen can represent sorrow, anger or joy seems astonishing. We must learn to exploit this unique property of the schematic drawing which gives it an incomparable advantage over x's and y's.

Masks

We shall now use another "dimension" to represent inter-actions. Let X be as in Figure 4.9 from the position of the external observer, and let him wish to appear in the eyes of others as shown in Figure 4.10.

Figure 4.9   Figure 4.10

Let X create his image in a special way and present it to people around him. We shall represent such a persona by attaching a mask to his true image (Figure 4.11).

Figure 4.11

Let Y be a member of the audience to which the mask is presented, and let the mask perform its function. That is to say, it is assimilated by Y as an image of X. This procedure is pictured in Figure 4.12.

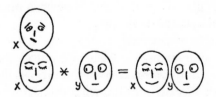

Figure 4.12

The "multiplication" is performed on the line. Elements above the line are not assimilated by the perceiver.

Figure 4.13 shows a case where the mask failed to function. Here X has assimilated X's true image and, moreover, the fact that a mask was superimposed on it.

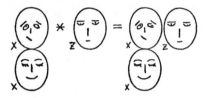

Figure 4.13

The concept of a mask is reflexively recursive. We can conceive of "a mask of a mask," "a mask of a mask of a mask," etc. Corresponding constructions are shown in Figure 4.14.

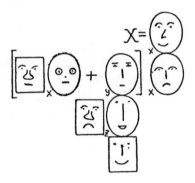

Figure 4.14

Y supposes that he has not only assimilated the true face of X, but has also discovered that X wears a mask. In reality, he has assimilated the mask; the face that he took to be a mask was a mask of a mask.

There is an interesting case where a persona shows a mask with the intention of making his audience think that "in reality" he is different and that what every one sees as reality is only a mask. In Figure 4.15, the top and bottom faces are identical.

Figure 4.15

The Iconic Sign, Ambiguity and Decision

Cartoon faces are only one of many kinds of signs that can be included in mathematical structures to register expression. We could utilize profiles, musical notation, or any abstract symbolism. We shall call such signs iconic.

By means of iconic signs traditional problems can be reformulated. They enable us to register ambiguity. First, note that faces make it possible to denote things more universal than behavioral acts or decisions. We do not know what the face in Figure 4.16 is "thinking about," nor the decision it

Figure 4.16

will reach. Such a question is meaningless since we have not defined a situation in which the expression of the face acquires a definite meaning and so makes it possible to speak of behavior and decision. However, having defined a situation, we can, within its framework, foretell decisions of a persona or guess actions already performed. Also, by immersing the face into different situations, we shall obtain different decisions. But the "indecisiveness" that characterizes this face will be manifested in all situations.

Suppose we are introduced to personae X, Y, Z, and U and are told that one of them is a murderer. We are invited to assign subjective probabilities that any of these personae is the murderer. Let the probability distribution be as shown in Table 2.

TABLE 2

X	Y	Z	U
0.1	0.2	0.6	0.1

Now suppose that instead of the symbols 0.1, 0.2, 0.6, 0.1, we resort to the faces in Figure 4.17.

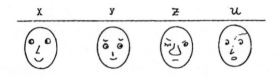

Figure 4.17

If the reader does not resist the force of suggestion in our example, Z will be the principal suspect. The faces have "selective power" with respect to a given set of actions. They seem to attract distinct types of human behavior. The set of faces governs our internal perception of likelihood. The traditional conception of probability is just one way of relating to reality and of perceiving likelihood. A set of faces is another way.

Ambivalence appears in a more stark form when instead of numerical distributions we make use of psychographic signs. One might object that for different investigators the degree of likelihood that Z is the murderer will be different. This is so, but this is the very criterion of ambivalence. The fact that the degree of conviction that Z is the killer is not constant speaks for our ability to reflect in notation our fluctuating evaluation that arose when we were studying the real suspects. In recent times we have been mesmerized by the notion of mathematical probability. We attempt to reduce all forms of ambivalence to it. The above example with the faces should not be reduced to the usual probability distribution (although this can be done very simply). The set of faces is the final form in which indeterminacy can be presented to the investigator.

In the following example, psychographic signs will be used to predict decisions. It is desired to represent a single interaction of Petrov and Sidorov (whom I know well) in a matrix game. Petrov chooses a row, Sidorov a column.

Sidorov's Choices

		S_2	T_2
Petrov's Choices	S_1	$-2, -2$	$-5, +3$
	T_2	$+5, -3$	$-10, -10$

To predict the outcome of the game, I must write down the reflexive polynomials of the players. From my position, Petrov is as shown in Figure 4.18. He usually shows a mask of a mild, somewhat timid man (Figure 4.19). Sidorov is straightforward and decisive (Figure 4.20). Apparently he does not assimilate his own image in the consciousness of others.

Figure 4.18   Figure 4.19   Figure 4.20

The interaction situation can be represented as follows.

a)   Sidorov assimilates Petrov.

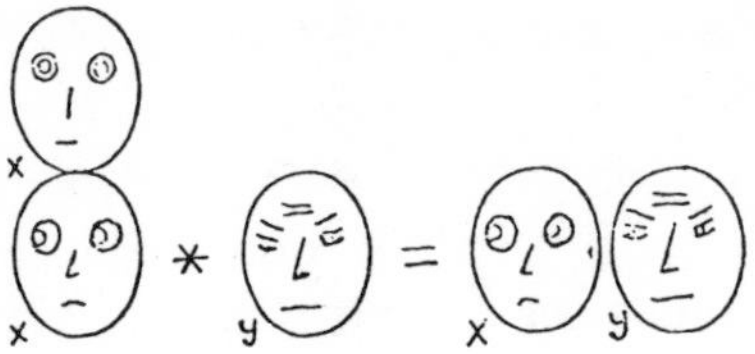

Figure 4.21

b) Petrov assimilates Sidorov. Since Petrov wears a mask, he has an image of himself as seen by others. The act of awareness is represented in Figure 4.22.

Figure 4.22

By observing Petrov's and Sidorov's reflexive portraits, I must deduce their decisions. Sidorov has only Petrov's mask in his inner world. It appears to *me* that Petrov, as he is seen from Sidorov's position, will choose S_1 while Sidorov will, on this basis, choose T_2. It appears to me that Petrov has assimilated the real Sidorov, hence should anticipate the latter's choice. Being indifferent toward Sidorov, he will not retaliate at the cost of a larger loss, hence Petrov will choose S_1. [See translator's note, page 107.]

Since I am acquainted with both men, I did not have to write down their polynomials in the cartoon-face notation. The method of representation is useful when I wish to communicate my findings and "feelings" to another investigator. I may not even know what game is presented to Petrov and Sidorov. But my representation enables another investigator to organize his intuition. Without knowing either Petrov or Sidorov, basing his deduction only on the notation that I communicated to him on a certain level of mutual understanding among investigators, this method of representing the players may be effective. Essentially, the indeterminacy of decisions in a game situation is annotated psychographically instead of in terms of probabilities.

In concluding this chapter, I offer an analysis of a poem by the great Russian poet Lermontov, one that is characterized by a remarkable reflexive structure. Note that assertions like "I know this" or "I feel this" are represented by Figure 4.23.

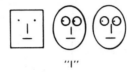

"I"

Figure 4.23

The "I" is the persona's reflection of himself. Therefore, the external observer must picture the position from which this "I" is fixated. On the other hand, to assertions like "He knows this" corresponds a structure of just two elements since self-reflection does not appear from the position of the external observer:

"He"

Figure 4.24

The polynomial is written vertically to the right of the poem, and an element of it corresponds to each line of the poem. Even a cursory glance at the connections between the polynomial and the text shows how the description of nature has been fused with the description of the characters. Note that there is no line that is connected to more than two elements of the polynomial.

Reflexive analysis enables us to single out reflexive structures in almost any fragment of culture and then to compare them. The investigator of social phenomena must assume a relation of parity to the culture he studies; otherwise he will

The Dream

In mid-day heat in Dagestan Valley,   1.

I lay motionless with lead in my breast.   2.

My deep wound was still open;   3.

Blood streamed from it.   4.

I lay alone on the sand of the valley   5.

Among rocky crags.   6.

The sun burned their yellow summits;   7.

And it burned me, but I slept the
                    sleep of the dead.   8.

I dreamt of a banquet lit by torches   9.

In the evening in my native land.   10.

And young women adorned with flowers   11.

Talked merrily about me.   12.

Not joining in the lively conversation,   13.

One sat lost in thought   14.

And her young soul was immersed   15.

God knows how into a sad dream.   16.

She dreamt of a valley in Dagestan.   17.

A corpse she knew lay there   18.

With an open black wound,   19.

From which cooling blood was streaming.   20.

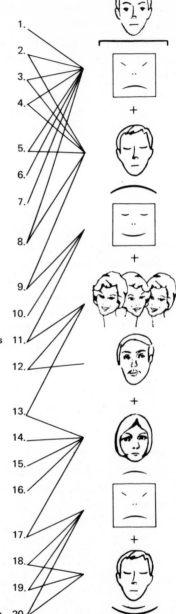

Figure 4.25

not understand the meaning of the elements. Thus, to take a stand over and above a culture, the investigator should submit to it.

We can distinguish two positions that can be assumed by an investigator: a dominant position and a parity position. Mathematical structures "serve" the dominant position; psychographic signs serve the parity position. It seems to me that mathematics, claiming a role in research on human cultures, should include the psychographics as an organic element.

Translator's note: The author's reasoning eludes me here. Perhaps another example will make the point. The illustrative game used is known in gaming literature as "Chicken" and in diplo-military circles as "brinkmanship." The "reflexive dynamics" of this game are such that if one player, say, Petrov (who chooses the horizontal rows) believes the other, Sidorov (who chooses the vertical columns) to be reckless or just plain crazy, then Petrov must choose the cautious strategy (S_1) for fear that Sidorov may well choose the reckless strategy (T_2). Suppose now Petrov is really a timid person, but wanting Sidorov to believe that he is a reckless person, puts on an appropriate mask. Next, suppose Petrov believes that Sidorov sees the mask, not the real Petrov. Then Petrov may think it is safe to play T_1 and "win," since Sidorov, seeing Petrov's mask will think that Petrov, being reckless, will choose T_1, in which case Sidorov's choice of T_2 leads to disaster. Suppose, however, that Sidorov sees the real Petrov but *has not replicated Petrov's reasoning.* Believing (correctly) that Petrov is a timid person, Sidorov believes that Petrov will play safe and choose S_1, which makes it safe for Sidorov to choose T_2. But Petrov chose T_1, not S_1. The result is disaster for both.

The advantages of inducing the opponent to believe that one is "crazy" have been frequently mentioned in the writings of American diplo-military strategists. See, for example, Daniel Ellsberg's Lowell Lectures, "The Art of Coercion: A Study of Threat in Economic Conflict and War." Lowell Institute, Boston, March, 1959. Also, Herman Kahn, *On Escalation.* New York: Praeger, 1965, p. 11.

Chapter 5

REFLEXIVE CONTROL

We shall now analyze interactions between personae, mainly in conflict situations. Consider a conflict in the framework of the reflexive polynomial

$$\Omega = T + Tx + (T + Tx)y.$$

Here the reality presented to Y is not only a representation of the arena but also a reflexion of his opponent's image of the arena. We shall suppose that within this framework Y has assimilated his opponent's goals and also his method of solving the problem—his "doctrine." Y faces the problem of controlling X's decision-process. The control is realized not via direct imposition of one's will on the opponent, but rather by supplying him with a "basis" for a decision predetermined by Y. Y "plugs himself into" X's reflecting system and so starts the control process. We have attempted to picture the situation in Figure 5.1.

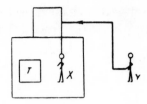

Figure 5.1

The process will be called *reflexive control* (Lefebvre, 1965a; 1966; 1967). Any deceptive movements, intrigues, camouflage, lies, etc. represent types of reflexive control, of which the illustrations in Figure 5.1 capture only the simplest features.

A lie may have a complex structure. For example, the opponent may be given true information in the expectation that he will take it to be false and act in accordance with that supposition.

Reflexive Control as a Method of Obtaining Information

Evidently, if X can "plug himself into" a channel over which Z communicates to Y, he can obtain the information communicated and so "penetrate inside" Y (cf., Figure 5.2).

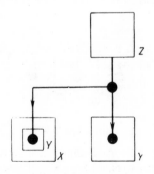

Figure 5.2

X can also plug himself into a channel over which Y transmits information obtained from Z (cf., Figure 5.3).

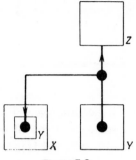

Figure 5.3

Finally, Y can simply give X the information in his possession (cf., Figure 5.4).

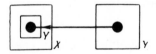

Figure 5.4

Besides these "natural" ways of "penetrating" Y, there is another. X can communicate to Y information that he has or that he has manufactured and insert it into his own image of Y (cf., Figure 5.5).

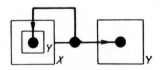

Figure 5.5

This last scheme, although apparently trivial, is paradoxical. Communication flows from X to Y, while information "flows" in the opposite direction. X receives information because he is *sending* a communication.

The information communicated may be about the arena, about the persona himself, about his point of view concerning the other's point of view, etc. What is important is that after information has been transmitted, X will be in possession of information about the other. In Chapter 6 we shall show how the principle of reflexive control can be realized in simple game-playing automata.

Reflexive control is a "strategic" method of getting information about the other. This, however, is only a part of the problem. Knowledge of the inner world of the other, regardless of its relation to reality can be of intrinsic value to X; but to the extent that the simplest types of reflexive control affect decisions, we must identify the components of decision processes and establish connections among them, however roughly.

A Representation of the Simplest Decision-Process

Let a persona be represented by the polynomial

$$\Omega = T + Tx.$$

We now extend the meaning of Tx to include not only the reflection of the arena, which we shall henceforth denote by M, but also the operative elements required to make a decision. We emphasize that the choice of these elements can be made in different ways, depending on the problem to be solved and the degree of detail required.

Suppose the arena consists of a number of sites and X's goal is to make deliveries to these sites by a single trip of a truck. The arena is assimilated by X, giving rise to the element Mx. We introduce the term "map" to denote a system of means used to identify the "objective situation." Clearly, this reflection can take place with different degrees of precision. For instance, some sites may be omitted, their configuration may be distorted, superfluous sites may be included, etc. However, X will now operate with Mx, not with T. Therefore, his decision will be based on Mx and only then applied more or less successfully to the arena.

X's goal is Gx, namely, to make the deliveries from some point A to all the sites in M by one trip. To decide on a plan to fulfill this goal, X must perform a certain operation on his map. We shall suppose that X possesses a definite method of solving the problem. We shall call this method his *doctrine,* denoted by Dx. Linear programming may be one such method, using a random device another, etc. We shall suppose that X's method is that of finding the shortest path for making the deliveries. The resulting path is entered upon the perceived map Mx.

Thus, the decision-process consists of the following steps.

(1) The goal is related to the map. Roughly speaking, the goal is "entered" upon the map. We symbolize this step by $\dfrac{Gx}{Mx}$.

(2) The doctrine is applied to the map with the goal entered upon it. This is symbolized by $\dfrac{Gx}{Mx}$ Dx.

(3) The result is a strategy Sx, related to Mx: $\dfrac{Gx}{Mx}$ Dx $\supset \dfrac{Sx}{Mx}$.

Now suppose X's opponent Y is represented by the polynomial $T + (T + Tx)y$. The entire situation is represented by

$$\Omega = T + Tx + (T + Tx)y.$$

We examine Y's decision-process, supposing that Y wants to capture X's truck. The ambush can be set only in the vicinity of B (say, in a forest); but to do this, one must know from which direction the truck will approach B. About this Y has no information. To make his decision, Y must replicate X's reasoning and arrive at X's decision. To replicate X's reasoning, Y must perform the following procedure:

$$\frac{Gx}{Mx} \; Dx \supset \frac{Sx}{Mx}.$$

However, Y does not have Mx. He has only what could be called Mx from Y's position. Moreover, Y knows neither X's goal Gx, nor X's doctrine Dx. All he has is the corresponding elements from his own position. Thus, Y's "replication" of X's reasoning takes place as

$$\frac{Gxy}{Mxy} \; Dxy \supset \frac{Sxy}{Mxy}.$$

Suppose Y assumes that X's doctrine is that of finding the optimal path by inspection. Suppose further that Y has assimilated the arena in a way different from X's and that Y knows X's map (say, through spies). Next, suppose also that Y assumes that his own image of the arena is correct. After

obtaining $\dfrac{Sxy}{Mxy}$, Y must enter his decision on his own map:

$$\frac{Sxy}{Mxy} \rightarrow \frac{Sxy}{My}.$$

Now Y must superpose a goal on his own map and apply his own doctrine, which amounts to marking the spot on the representation of the route along which X should (from Y's point of view) arrive at B. This is where Y will set his ambush. In this way, Y obtains his own decision:

$$\frac{Sxy}{My} \rightarrow \frac{Sxy \; Gy}{My} \; Dy \supset \frac{Sy}{My}.$$

Combining the above into a single expression, we get a generalized symbolic representation of the decision process in this situation:

$$\frac{Gxy}{Mxy} \; Dxy \supset \frac{Sxy}{Mxy} \; \rightarrow \; \frac{Sxy}{My} \; \rightarrow \; \frac{Sxy \; Gy}{My} \; Dy \supset \frac{Sy}{My} \; .$$

It can be easily seen that to the extent that X's reasoning can be replicated, his attempt to optimize may lead to his defeat.

Let us now derive X's decision process, supposing that it is represented by the polynomial $T + [T + (T + Tx)y]$ x. Analysis analogous to the above leads to the chain:

$$\frac{Gxyx}{Mxyx} \; Dxyx \supset \frac{Sxyx}{Mxyx} \; \rightarrow \; \frac{Sxyx}{Myx} \; \rightarrow \; \frac{Sxyx \; Gyx}{Myx} \; Dyx \supset$$

$$\frac{Syx}{Myx} \; \rightarrow \; \frac{Syx}{Mx} \; \rightarrow \; \frac{Syx \; Gx}{Mx} \; Dx \supset \frac{Sx}{Mx}$$

The general method of constructing formulae based on arbitrary polynomials of this type is easy to discern.

Two types of reality reflexion described by the polynomial $\Omega = T + Tx$ are to be noted. In one type, the persona reflecting reality is not included in the arena (cf., Figure 5.6). Here there is a distinction between Mx on the one hand and

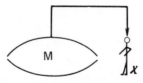

Figure 5.6

the elements Dx and Gx on the other. Gx appears as a particular function of the reflected relation of self as an actor to the arena. Since this kind of reflexion does not establish that relation, the goal cannot be reflected. It appears, instead, as a sort of "intention." In other words, the awareness of one's goal as one's own is possible only when one's own actions or one's own relations to the object are perceived. This perception transforms the "intention" into a goal.

In general, the very conception of a goal already contains the sense of "perceived intention." The goal appears only as a specific reflexive formation in a teleological construction. Evidently, it makes no sense to speak of the goals of a bee or an ant.

V. I. Dubovskaya proposed to describe this type of reflexion by

$$\Omega = T + \dot{T}x,$$

where the dot over the T symbolizes the absence of self as a substantive construct in X's inner world. In the other type of reflexion, the persona includes his own body and his actions into his image of the arena (cf., Figure 5.7). Here he can assimilate his relation to the object, and the intention becomes a goal.

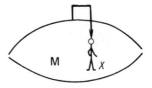

Figure 5.7

Dealing with a doctrine is more complicated. If the persona can become aware of it, he distinguishes between his image of reality and reality. The simplest polynomial in which such a distinction can take place has the form

$$T + (T + Tx)x.$$

Thus, when the terms Txx and Tyy are absent, we are less than precise if we suppose that our personae have the elements Dx and Dy. We have sacrificed precision to simplify the discussion.

Reflexive Control in Conflict with
$\Omega = T + Tx + (T + Tx)y$

In this context, reflexive control can be generally written in the form of the transformation

$$Txy \rightarrow Tx.$$

Here Txy is a planned element, not a reflected one. This can be taken into account by time indices:

$$Tx_{i+j}y_i \rightarrow Tx_{i+j}.$$

That is, the element Tx at time i+j from Y's position is transformed at time i into Tx at time i+j. Put in another way, $Tx_{i+j}y_i$ is some "future" planned in the present. For simplicity we shall drop the time indices.

In a conflict taking place within the framework of the above polynomial, reflexive control can be realized by means of any of the following transformations:

$$Mxy \rightarrow Mx$$

$$Gxy \rightarrow Gx$$

$$Dxy \rightarrow Dx$$

$$Sxy \rightarrow Sx.$$

Constructing an image of the arena (Mxy → Mx). This is one of the most common methods of control. Camouflage is an example. The purpose of camouflage is to give the opponent information, not to deprive him of it. The information given to the opponent is "There is nothing here."

Constructing the opponent's goal (Gxy → Gx). Provocation is the most common variant of this type of control. It may be realized through "ideological sabotage," treacherous "friendly advice," etc. An example is the puerile prank of putting a banknote in a conspicuous place with a concealed thread attached. The prank often succeeds, affording satisfaction to the organizers.

Constructing the opponent's doctrine (Dxy → Dx). The opponent's doctrine is a particular tool for making decisions, in the simplest case an algorithm for deducing a strategy from the way the map is structured. Sometimes the doctrine takes the form of a primitive prescription like "if a > b, choose a." The opponent's doctrine is imposed on the opponent by teaching him. For example, suppose a soccer player, using a certain systematic line of attack is confronted with a certain counteraction by one of the defenders. The fact that the defender's action has become stereotyped can be utilized by the attacker at a decisive moment.

The connection (Mxy → Mx) ⊃ (Gxy → Gx). In armed conflict, goals are distinguished by different degrees of importance. A "global goal," may be that of crushing the opponent and taking possession of his territory. This goal may be formulated before the start of the conflict and preserved to the end. A limited goal of a comparatively small unit of an attacking force may be to reach a given line of defence, to capture a town, or the like. These limited goals arise during the conflict as a result of some local situation reflected on the map. One of the parties can deduce the goal from the image of the arena on the map (Mx → Gx) and so construct a system of reflexive control. For instance, by weakening one of his flanks in a way that permits the opponent to enter this on his map, Y can give X a basis for deducing a goal, say to occupy a certain line.

Y acts as follows: First he formulates the desired element Gxy. Then he selects an Mxy from which Gxy can be deduced. The actions directed at the transformation Mxy → Mx are undertaken next. Now X begins to act. He deduces Gx from Mx. The resulting chain is

$$Gxy \supset Mxy \rightarrow Mx \supset Gx.$$

Here the transformation Gxy → Gx is performed by means of the transformation Mxy → Mx. This type of control is conveniently represented thus:

$$(Mxy \to Mx) \supset (Gxy \to Gx).$$

In most real conflicts the map cannot be transmitted to the opponent in its entirety. Usually, the opponent is supplied with a set of "bench marks" from which he constructs his image of the arena. One starts with the assumption that the opponent uses some fixed deductive procedure. For instance, in the second millenium B.C., Gideon used torches as a means of reflexive control over his enemy, the Midianite army (Linebarger, 1954). According to the logistic norms of that time, one trumpeter and one torch bearer were assigned to each 100 soldiers. Gideon assumed that this norm was known to the Midianite leaders and that they were familiar at least with the rudiments of arithmetic. Gideon equipped each one of his soldiers with a torch and a trumpet. He assumed that the enemy would conclude that an army of 30,000 was arrayed against him and would deduce a goal, namely to avoid battle. (As we are told, the Midianites in fact ran.) The situation is schematized thus:

Gideon's reasoning   The Midianites' reasoning

$$Gxy \supset Mxy \supset Sxy \longrightarrow Sx \supset Mx \supset Gx$$

Actually, a goal was induced in the opponent; but this was done via inducing an image of the arena, and this image was induced by transmitting some "bench marks." This type of control can be represented thus:

$$(Sxy \to Sx) \supset (Mxy \to Mx) \supset (Gxy \to Gx).$$

Conflict with $\Omega = T + (T + Tx)y +$
$[T + (T + Tx)y] x$

Here X can potentially construct a system of reflexive control governed by the transformation $(T + Tx)yx \to (T + Tx)y$. That is, the following transformation can take place:

$$Tyx \quad \to \quad Ty$$

$$Txyx \quad \to \quad Txy$$

We expand the last of these transformations:

$$Mxyx \quad \to \quad Mxy$$

$$Gxyx \quad \to \quad Gxy$$

$$Dxyx \quad \to \quad Dxy$$

Control via $Mxyx \to Mxy$. The opponent is given what appears as his own view of the arena. The transmittal can be accomplished by a deliberate deposition of documents. Besides, there may be a "confirmation" to the effect that the opponent's camouflage has not been discovered, say that the false objects constructed by him have been mistaken for real ones, all of this being false information.

Control via $Gxyx \to Gxy$. An example is a basketball player's maneuver, wherein he feints a movement to the left to give the impression that he intends to by-pass the opponent on that side, whereupon he by-passes him on the right.

Control via $Dxyx \to Dxy$. Let X be a pursuer armed with a pistol and Y his quarry. Y runs into a cave with six exits (cf., Figure 5.8). X can shoot Y only if Y chooses an exit in the line of fire from the exit taken by X. The situation is depicted in Figure 5.9. Each arrow is a possible line of fire. X's strategy is to let Y know that he (X) will choose his exit by throwing a die. Let Y's doctrine consist of calculating the

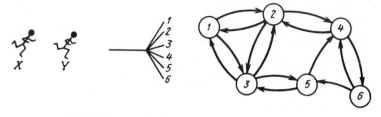

Figure 5.8   Figure 5.9

probabilities of being shot at each of the exits and in choosing the exit with the minimal probability. If X's choices are equiprobable, Y will choose exit 6, where the probability of being shot is smallest. Actually, however, X does not intend to throw a die. He deduces the quarry's choice of exit 6 from the quarry's *assumption* that X will throw a die. Thus X takes exit 4 and wins.

Many types of reflexive control are of this sort. If X and Y are two opposing armies, many combat operations performed by X fulfill two functions: on the one hand as an impact on Y, on the other hand, the configuration of X's combat forces must represent a particular "text," which, when read by the opponent must (as X intends) lead him to certain conclusions about X's goals. The chain of deductions and transformations has the form

$$Gxyx \supset Mxyx \rightarrow Mxy \supset Gxy.$$

If one's goal is communicated to the opponent by presenting him with one's own image of the arena, we shall represent this type of reflexive control by

$$(Mxyx \rightarrow Mxy) \supset (Gxyx \rightarrow Gxy).$$

For example, X concentrates his artillery not for the purpose of attacking Y but in order to induce Y to conclude that X intends to attack. Here X utilizes a considerable portion of his forces to create a "text" out of his own "body" addressed to the opponent. There are circumstances when X cannot prevent the adequate transformation Mx → Mxy. Then Y can often discover X's goal, deducing it from Mxy.

To prevent the discovery of his true goal, X can attempt to choose a subgoal, the realization of which, when discovered by Y would permit X to deduce several equiprobable goals, among which the real goal is concealed:

$$(Mx \rightarrow Mxy) \supset Gx \rightarrow \begin{cases} G^1xy \\ G^2xy \\ \cdot \\ \cdot \\ \cdot \\ G^nxy \end{cases}$$

The German breakthrough at Sedan, May 15, 1940, is an example of such an operation. B. H. Lidell-Hart describes it as follows (Lidell-Hart, 1941, p. 305):

> The rapid progress of the German penetration beyond Sedan benefited much from the fact that it successively threatened alternative objectives, and kept the French in doubt as to its real direction—first whether it was towards Paris or the rear of the forces in Belgium; then, when the German armoured divisions swung westwards, whether they were moving on Amiens or Lille. Selling the dummy first one way and then the other, they swept on to the Channel coast.

The choice of the center as the breakthrough point was explained as an attempt to conceal the true goal, namely, an advance toward the English Channel. The Germans (X) could not conceal the actual movement of their tanks from the French (Y). That is, the transformation Mx → Mxy was unavoidable. But Mx was chosen in such a way as to indicate two equiprobable goals:

$$\text{Advance toward the Channel} \supset Mx \to Mxy \supset \begin{cases} \text{Advance on Paris} \\ \\ \text{Advance toward} \\ \text{Channel} \end{cases}$$

This is why the French command was put in a difficult position.

In the framework of the polynomial

$$\Omega = T + (T + Tx)y + [T + (T + Tx)y] \, x,$$

both X and Y exercise reflexive control. Y can strive to realize the following transformations:

$$Mxy \to Mx$$

$$Gxy \to Gx$$

$$Dxy \to Dx.$$

However, to the extent that X replicates Y's inner world and can deduce the possibility of reflexive control, Y's attempt can lead to failure. Suppose Y is convinced that he has exercised reflexive control successfully. He assumes that he has induced in X an image of the arena, a goal, and a doctrine, and so is supposedly informed about X's inner world. In working out his strategy, Y begins to utilize the elements Mxy, Gxy, and Dxy. His reflexive control fails, however, because Y has revealed to X the elements that enter his strategic calculations, and so has actually simplified X's problem. Instead of the transformations planned by Y, the following transformations took place:

$$Mxy \to Mxyx$$

$$Gxy \to Gxyx$$

$$Dxy \to Dxyx.$$

X, having obtained vital information, can reconstruct his own image, as it appears to Y. X can exercise effective control by convincing Y that the transformations which X tried to bring about actually took place. Moreover, X can potentially perform the following additional transformations:

$$Myx \rightarrow My$$

$$Gyx \rightarrow Gy$$

$$Dyx \rightarrow Dy$$

The following is the possible scheme of mutual induction:

X	Gx	Dx	Mx	Gyx	Dyx	Myx	Gxyx	Dxyx	Mxyx
				↓	↓	↓	↑	↑	↑
Y				Gy	Dy	My	Gxy	Dxy	Mxy

If Y does not perform the reflexive control uncovered by X, there are no upward arrows, and X must construct his system of control as follows:

X	Gx	Dx	Mx	Gyx	Dyx	Myx	Gxyx	Dxyx	Mxyx
				↓	↓	↓	↓	↓	↓
Y				Gy	Dy	My	Gxy	Dxy	Mxy

Thus, failure of reflexive control may be an instance of imparting valuable information to the opponent.

Note that in the framework of the polynomial

$$\Omega = T + (T + Tx)y + [T + (T + Tx)y] \, x,$$

X and Y perform reflexive control of which neither is aware. Consider Y. He may attempt to perform the transformation $Txy \rightarrow Tx$, but Txy is not present in his inner world. Therefore he cannot replicate the preceding transformation ($Txy \rightarrow Tx$)y. Analogously, X cannot replicate the transformation

Txyx → Txy, since Txyx is missing from his inner world. (This element exists only from the position of the external observer.) It follows that the personae cannot be aware of the types of reflexive control exercised by them. (The author's attention was called to this point by V. E. Lepsky and P. V. Baranov.)

The minimal polynomial that enables the personae to plan the above transformation is

$$\Omega = \ T + (T + Tx + Txy)y +$$

$$[T + Ty + Tyx + Txy + Txyx] \ x.$$

Using Baranov's notation, where arrows replace certain plus signs, we write

$$\Omega = \ T + [T + (Tx \leftarrow Txy)]y +$$

$$[T + (Ty \leftarrow Tyx) + (Txy \leftarrow Txyx)] \ x,$$

where the possibility of consciously planned reflexive control is apparent.

Evidently, awareness of reflexive control is not necessary for its realization. Therefore we examine simpler polynomials in the framework of which there is no such awareness. More complex schemes of reflexive control involving more complex polynomials can be analyzed analogously.

Maneuvers

Schemes of reflexive control developed in time form a distinct class. In some instances, one opponent transmits to the other his "pseudohistory," in order to induce him to extrapolate it and so to deduce a prognosis, credible from his position, of the future state of self and to choose a strategy based on this prognosis. An example is a sudden change in a pattern of activity. We shall describe some experimental studies related to this form of control in Chapter 6.

Artificial Construction of Reflexive
Structures and of
Operators of Awareness

It seems that the most developed method of control is the construction of the reflexive structure of the persona to be controlled. The simplest of this sort of construction is that of "planting" a specific polynomial in the persona to be controlled. When X tells Y that Z is interested in Y's view of the situation in an arena T, he constructs the polynomial

$$\Omega = T + (T + Ty + Tyz)y.$$

This polynomial can determine a whole class of strategy choices by Y. Essentially, X predetermines the form of the information required by Y to make decisions. We stress the fact that whereas we previously spoke of reflexive control as an influence over the other's decision-making, assuming that the actor who exercises control knows the reflexive polynomial of the other, we now speak of reflexive control as directed at the polynomial itself.

A more effective form of reflexive control involves the insertion of an operator of awareness in the other, that is, an influence over the other's very screen of consciousness. Essentially, if the process is successful, the persona under control is confined to a narrow class of polynomials, and his decisions will be predicted with considerable accuracy by the controller.

Chapter 6

DEVICES THAT TURN

APPREHENSIONS INTO REALITY

It is very difficult to study reflexive control directly in the context of human conflicts. It is, therefore, useful to create special automata that can realize various schemes of control. We call such automata *dribblings*. These can be regarded as measuring devices by means of which certain objective characteristics of human reflexion can be examined. It turned out that it is possible to build automata exhibiting a paradoxical feature: They work better when a person tries to interfere with their operation than when they are left to themselves.

Imagine a city as a maze of streets intersecting in squares. A traveler starting at the center seeks a way out. We assume that he does not recognize the streets or the squares, that is, has no memory. Next, suppose that the traveler upon arriving at a square asks directions to the nearest exit and that the inhabitants have conspired to detain him in the city as long as possible. An experiment conducted by the author (Lefebvre,

1967; 1969b) shows that if the traveler is modeled by a very simple automaton, able to exercise reflexive control, while a human subject plays the part of the inhabitants, the traveler can find his way out of the maze more quickly than if he wandered around without paying attention to the instructions.

A System Working Against Interference

Our device consists of three blocks (cf., Figure 6.1). The first is a map of the maze with green and yellow light bulbs at each intersection. Five nodes on the periphery are exits.

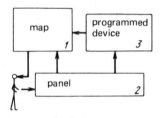

Figure 6.1

The subject's task is to prevent the "traveler" from leaving the maze. The traveler's motion is represented by the changing position of an activated yellow light. He does not know the location of the exits and has no memory. He makes his moves only after receiving instructions given to him by the subject pressing buttons on a panel (the second block). The traveler can move from a node only to adjacent nodes. The subject sees the instructions which he gives to the traveler as a green light. These instructions are transmitted to the third block, a programmed device that controls the traveler's moves.[8]

The program is designed as follows: At each node the traveler can react to the subject's instructions in two ways: either follow the instruction or move to an "opposite" node. The programmed device contains a table of opposite nodes (the relation of opposition is not, in general, symmetric). The program can be represented by a series of integers with alternating signs. We have used the following program:

```
+5  −6  +2  −4  +4  −1  +1  −2  +4  −3  +2  −1  +1  −3
+4  −3  +4  −2  +1  −1  +3  −2  +3  −4  +2  −1  +5  −3.
```

The sign attached to each integer indicates the traveler's reaction, "+" meaning following an instruction, "−" meaning choosing the opposite node. Table 3 shows pairs of opposite

TABLE 3

2	1 − 10 10 − 1 3 − 5 5 − 3	11	4 − 18 8 − 19 18 − 4 19 − 8	18	11 − 17 14 − 23 17 − 11 23 − 14	3	2 − 8 8 − 2 4 − 6 6 − 4
12	6 − 13 7 − 16 13 − 15 15 − 13 16 − 7	19	9 − 23 11 − 26 23 − 9 26 − 11	4	1 − 11 11 − 1 3 − 9 9 − 3	13	7 − 17 12 − 14 14 − 16 16 − 7 17 − 12
20	5 − 21 10 − 24 21 − 5 24 − 10	6	3 − 12 12 − 3 7 − 10 10 − 7	14	7 − 17 8 − 17 13 − 18 17 − 8 18 − 13	21	15 − 25 25 − 15 20 − 22 22 − 20
7	14 − 6 6 − 13 8 − 13 12 − 8 13 − 6	15	10 − 16 16 − 10 12 − 21 21 − 12	22	16 − 23 23 − 16 17 − 21 21 − 17	8	3 − 14 14 − 3 11 − 7 7 − 11
16	12 − 17 13 − 22 15 − 17 17 − 15 22 − 13	23	18 − 25 25 − 18 19 − 22 22 − 19	10	2 − 15 6 − 20 20 − 6 15 − 2	17	13 − 22 14 − 16 16 − 18 18 − 16 22 − 13
				25	21 − 26 26 − 21 24 − 23 23 − 24		

NOTE: The number to the left of each column designates the node at which the traveler may be. The first number in each column designate adjacent nodes; the second number designate the nodes called "opposite."

nodes. The magnitude of each integer designates the number of consecutive instructions which are to be obeyed or disobeyed. This program was chosen as a result of a pilot experiment and, once adopted, was no longer changed. The problem to be solved by this device is to move the traveler to one of the exits.

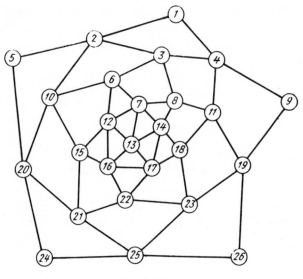

Figure 6.2

Figure 6.2 represents the maze. The traveler is initially at node 13. Nodes 1, 5, 9, 24, and 26 are the exits. The subject sits in front of the maze map. The experimenter gives him the following instructions:

You see a maze. A traveler is represented by a point in it. (Node 13 lights up.) The point can move along the lines connecting the nodes. (The point moves to an adjacent node and returns to 13.) The traveler's task is to leave the maze through one of the gates. He does not know where the gates are and does not remember where he has been. You may give him directions by lighting a green lamp. (A green lamp lights up a neighboring node.) Your task is to keep the point within the maze as long as possible. You win if you keep it for twenty-five moves; otherwise it wins. Treat the point as you would a person who is trying to escape and whose escape you are trying to prevent.

Some subjects ask how the point reacts to instructions. The experimenter replies that he does not know; that the program is "welded" into the device, but that in principle the point behaves as it pleases. Thereupon the game begins. There are no time limits on the subject's decisions. The experimenter records every run, including the subject's instructions and the point's reactions.

Thirty-two students of Moscow Engineering Institute participated as subjects, each of whom played twice. The distributions of the number of moves made in the first and second runs is shown in Table 4. All runs lasted until the traveler reached an exit.

TABLE 4

					Distribution of the Numbers of Moves in First Runs						
Number of moves	7	8	9	10	11	15	16	17	25	37	39	46
Number of runs	0	4	5	6	4	4	4	1	1	1	1	1

					Distribution of the Numbers of Moves in Second Runs										
Number of moves	7	8	9	10	11	12	16	17	19	27	28	29	39	52	56	75
Number of runs	1	6	8	2	2	1	2	2	1	1	1	1	1	1	1	1

The mean number of moves in the first runs turned out to be fifteen, in the second runs, eighteen. An empirical formula for the distributions can be constructed from these data.

The Device Working Without Interference

Here the subject is simulated by a digital computer, the node to which the traveler is instructed to move being chosen equiprobably from among the adjacent nodes. The traveler follows the program described above. Thus, the model can be interpreted as representing a traveler who at each move casts lots and either follows the direction indicated by the outcome or chooses the direction designated as "opposite" with equal probabilities. Since the relation "opposite" is not generally symmetric in our case (cf., Table 3), this strategy might result in a mean length of a run different from that in a random walk. It turns out that in our case, the difference is disadvantageous to the traveler. Specifically, the mean length of a run turns out to be twenty-seven moves, compared with twenty-five in a random walk.

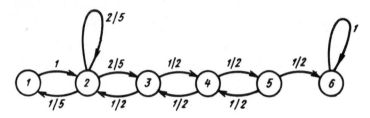

Figure 6.3

The random walk model is a six-state Markov chain. State 1 is node 13 (cf., Figure 6.3). State 2 consists of nodes 7, 12, 14, 16, 17; state 3 of nodes 6, 8, 22, 16, 18; state 4 of nodes 3, 10, 11, 21, 23; state 5 of nodes 2, 4, 19, 20, 25; state 6 (absorbing) consists of the exits, i.e., nodes 1, 5, 9, 24, 26. The Markov chain is represented by the matrix

$$A = (a_{ij}) = \begin{pmatrix} 0 & 1 & 0 & 0 & 0 & 0 \\ .2 & .4 & .4 & 0 & 0 & 0 \\ 0 & .5 & 0 & .5 & 0 & 0 \\ 0 & 0 & .5 & 0 & .5 & 0 \\ 0 & 0 & 0 & .5 & 0 & .5 \\ 0 & 0 & 0 & 0 & 0 & 1 \end{pmatrix}$$

By the well-known result on Markov chains, the probability that the system will be in the absorbing state after at most m transitions is given by the element a_{16} of A^m.

Comparison of Performance With and Without Interference

As we have seen, the mean number of moves to absorption in a random walk is twenty-five. With interference, the mean is fifteen in the first runs of each subject and eighteen in the second. The corresponding distributions are shown in Figure 6.4. Evidently, interference improves the performance.

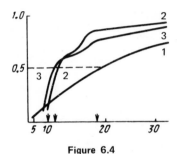

Figure 6.4

Comparing the medians, we have nineteen moves in the random walk, ten in the first runs, eleven in the second runs. A record of the runs is shown in Table 5.

TABLE 5

Level (state) indicated by subject	2	2	1	2	2	1	2	3	4
Node indicated by subject	7	14	13	16	12	13	16	15	3
Node to which "traveler" moved	7	14	13	16	12	15	10	2	5
Level to which "traveler" moved	2	2	1	2	2	3	4	5	6

The corresponding graph is shown in Figure 6.5.

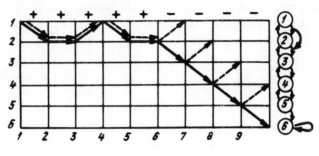

Figure 6.5

Causes of Improvement by Interference

Improvement results from the exercise of reflexive control by the program over the subject. In the first five moves, the program follows the subject's instructions. As shown in Figure 6.5, the dotted lines and the arrows coincide. The subject interprets these moves as "obedience" on the part of the traveler. When this conviction is established, the traveler begins to "exploit" it, choosing nodes opposite to those suggested. The traveler "knows" the subject's goal and is in possession of the image of his "own" doctrine in the mind of the subject. These data enable the traveler to orient his map, since from his point of view the subject gives him instructions that lead him away from his goal. Therefore if the traveler chooses opposite nodes, he will approach the gate. Clearly, the automaton does not reason this out. The reasoning was done by the programmer who wrote the sequence of numbers. As can be seen in Figure 6.5, after the first six moves, the subject attempted to guide the traveler toward the center and by this very attempt led him out of the maze.

Some subjects guessed the traveler's doctrine correctly after he stopped following instructions (namely that he chooses opposite nodes) and started to show him the way out with the intention of leading him back to the center.

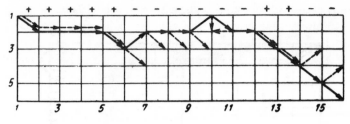

Figure 6.6

This is shown in the record depicted in Figure 6.6. After concluding that the traveler is obedient, the subject tried to put him into state 4 on the sixth move. But the traveler stopped obeying and went to state 2. The subject changed his conception about the traveler's doctrine. He was now convinced that the traveler would disobey and consequently started to suggest moves toward the periphery. Note that the realization of the traveler's disobedience is not yet sufficient to determine a plan of action. The subject must still determine the instructions to be given. (Most subjects failed to solve this problem.) After the twelfth move, the traveler again follows the subject's instructions, while the subject, using the strategy that he has worked out, inadvertently leads him to the periphery. Since the traveler is now obedient, the subject, who has spent two moves in discovering this, begins to suggest moves toward the center. But after move 14, the traveler again starts to disobey, and, to the extent that he has convinced the subject that he is obedient, he is enabled to escape.[9] The traveler's success is explained by the circumstance that he formulates the subject's behavior, utilizes it, and "overtakes" the subject.

In characterizing the subject's behavior, we have deliberately avoided the concept of learning, since we have no a priori information about the rate at which information is acquired. It would seem that in the context of an experiment of this sort, this rate is sufficiently standard. Note, further, that the automaton plays the subject without feedback from the subject's behavior. Thus, the traveler gets no information about whether he was successful or not.[10] The sequence of numbers that governs the traveler is a particular a priori model of the subject performing an act of awareness.

If we were to anthropomorphize the automaton, we would say that it has a model of the subject, including the latter's acts of awareness, leading to changes in his behavior. In this manner, the automaton can predict the subject's actions without having any information about them via feedback. Of course, we must remember that feedback was involved when the "a priori" model was being constructed during the pilot experiment. Nevertheless, in each particular experiment, the rigid algorithm was not influenced by the subject's behavior.

Next, note that the subject plays with an automaton. The "traveler" is a certain element in the subject's inner world, induced by the instructions. The experimenter's problem was to create an appropriate "gaming" world inside the subject by means of the instructions (which are themselves a sort of reflexive control). The subject is induced to see the light bulbs as a traveler; the maze as a city. In this version of the experiment, the experimenter must be excluded from the picture presented to the subject. We can, however, think of another experiment in which the subject knows that he is participating in an artificial situation (more precisely, his awareness of this circumstance becomes dominant) and moreover that he is playing against a rigid program built into the machine by the experimenter. Here the structure of the subject's inner world is, in principle, different.

We have performed a number of experiments of this kind. The subject (one of the experimenters in our group) knew that another experimenter was going to construct a program to play specially against him. The reflexive game is now a different one. The difference can be illustrated schematically as in Figures 6.7 and 6.8.

In the latter experiment, the designers of experiments can engage in a contest to decide who can guess more effectively the program constructed by the other. Each independently writes a program. Neither must see the performance of the

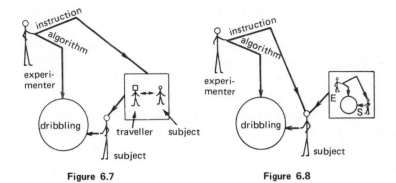

Figure 6.7   **Figure 6.8**

other; otherwise, by analyzing the other's manner of play he may intuitively reconstruct the algorithm presented to him. Contests of this sort may enable us to construct a graph in which each directed link represents superiority of one contestant over another.

The Baranov-Trudoliubov Experiments

In the first of these experiments (Baranov and Trudoliubov, 1969a, b), the subjects were presented with a diagram of a symmetric maze with two exits (cf., Figure 6.9).

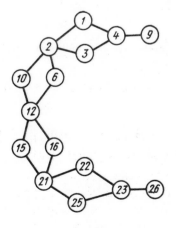

Figure 6.9

The subject was asked to select secretly one of the exits and to write down its number. The task was to prevent the traveler from escaping through that exit. As before, the algorithm was without feedback. The idea of the experiment was similar to that of the previous one. First, the traveler induced a conviction in the subject that he is obedient; then he utilized this conviction, induced the opposite one, induced this one, and so on. In this experiment, 72 percent of the runs ended in the traveler's escape through the exit that the subject tried to interdict.

The algorithm regulating the movement of the traveler was

+2   −3   +1   −3   +1   −2   +3   −1   +3   −1

The subjects were 10 female and 51 male students at the Moscow Energetic Institute. The ratio of losses to wins was 38:13 for males, 7:3 for females. The mean length of runs was 18 moves. The mean length of runs won by the automaton was 15; of those lost by the automaton, 26.5. The mean length of a random walk in this scheme is 25.[11]

In the second experiment, the subject chose secretly one of four goals.

(1) To lead the traveler out through exit 9 and to prevent his escape through exit 25.

(2) Vice versa.

(3) To lead the traveler out in a minimum number of moves, fewer than 25.

(4) To keep the traveler in the maze as long as possible, at least for 25 moves.

The program was independent of the goal chosen. The first algorithm used in a pilot experiment was

+2   −3   +1   −4   +1   −3   +3   −1   +4   −1   +1   −1

Subjects were students at the Lenin State Pedagogical Institute, Moscow. The results are shown in Table 6.

TABLE 6

	Problems				
	1	2	3	4	summary result
Number of runs	26	12	27	20	85
Ratio of dribbling's wins to losses	19 : 7	12 : 0	6 : 21	17 : 3	54 : 31

As is seen, the dribbling wins predominantly in all tasks except the third. Thereupon the algorithm was modified as follows:

+2   −3   +1   −4   +1   −3   +3   −2   +3   −1   +1   −1

In the next experiment, the subjects, instead of choosing a problem drew a number from a box. Actually all the numbers in the box were three. In these runs it was possible to utilize the results of the previous runs on problems 1, 2, and 4, since a substantial majority of these runs ended on the initial, unchanged portion of the algorithm, while the runs that went beyond this portion were counted as lost by the dribbling. The results of the second series are shown in Table 7.

TABLE 7

	Problems				
	1	2	3	4	summary result
Number of runs	26	12	39	20	97
Ratio of dribbling's wins to losses	18 : 8	10 : 2	22 : 17	18 : 2	68 : 29

The author considers the results important, since the experiment demonstrated the possibility of constructing an effective system of reflexive control more or less independent of the content of the experimental situation. Moreover, the situations were characterized by two different criteria of winning, namely, in two of the problems the number of moves, in the other two one of two alternatives. The experiment showed that it is possible to find a scheme of reflexive control relatively insensitive to the criterion. What is essential is the subject's opposition to the dribbling.

Dribblings that improve their performance in the face of opposition by human subjects can be regarded as devices that transform apprehension into reality. These devices, if left to themselves, either achieve certain states only rarely or are characterized by a constant distribution of final states. But if a human being acts to prevent the passage of the system to a given state, the system achieves this very state either more quickly or more probably.

Chapter 7

REFLEXIVE COMMUNICATION

IN GROUPS

*The Simplest Reflexive Model of
a Social Organism*

Let T be a material background for a developing reflexive conception. Let personae e_1, e_2, $\cdots$ e_n be included in T. Each persona has his own image of T: Te_1, Te_2, $\cdots$ Te_n. Moreover, the images in some of the personae can be assimilated by others, giving rise to elements $Te_1 e_j$ and so on. Thus we have the following symbolic representation of the system:

$$\Omega = T + \sum_i Te_i + \sum_i \sum_j Te_j e_i + \sum_i \sum_j \sum_k Te_k e_j e_i + \cdots$$

For some persona e_i some elements may be missing. The above development of Ω in series exhibits the global reflexive characterization of a social organism or of parts of it.

A system of intelligent beings will be characterized by the presence of at least the third term of the series,

$$\sum_i \sum_j Te_j e_i.$$

In some measure, the development of a civilization may be characterized by an increase in the number of terms required to describe it.

Eventually, space research will necessitate models of civilizations beyond the solar system. It seems to us that specific representability by a reflexive polynomial is the "universal" that enables us to identify civilizations as a class of systems. Civilizations differ fundamentally from other types of systems, such as cell colonies that constitute a living organism or colonies of individuals such as ant hills. An ant hill can be represented by the form $\Omega = T + \sum_i Te_i$, where Te_i is an image of the environment that enables each persona e_i to orient itself. As pointed out above, the system becomes a simplest civilization when the series takes the form

$$\Omega = T + \sum_i Te_i + \sum_i \sum_j Te_j e_i = T + \sum_i (T + \sum_j Te_j)e_i.$$

In systems containing terms of the second degree, human communication is possible and "spiritual values" may arise. The presence of reflexion does not always make a system more adaptive or perfect. We can imagine a community of quite primitive individuals, each no more developed than a bee. But if these individuals assimilate each other's images, if they are able to look at the world through each other's eyes, we must subsume such communities under civilizations. We can assume that reflexive structures are not connected to the way systems function. For instance, the use of tools is not a necessary component for realizing a reflexive polynomial in the "substance" of the system (see p. 160).

In general, any civilization or some subsystem of it can be represented in the form

$$\Omega = T + \sum_i \Omega_i e_i.$$

where Ω_i is the inner world of persona e_i. In this notation, the nature of this inner world defines a particular civilization. We now have a model to serve in the analysis of the reflexive structure of a social system.

We can express the reflexive inequality of different personae. Some, like motion picture stars are in everyone's inner world; others in only a few. We can analyze the variety of images within different personae and represent different depths of analysis. Finally, the symbolic representation reveals the realization of reflexive control. In particular, it becomes possible to pose the problem of external control if the investigator wants to bring the system into a given state. To the extent that the investigator is at times one of the personae, he must include his own reflexive images in the series. In this case, the free term T will become the image Te_i, where e_i is the investigator. The problem of reflexive control will consist of the effect on the fixed terms of the series. Possibly, in further development, the model will serve to establish some relation of the free term to the other terms and so to describe the evolution of the whole system. It may be possible to explain the function of various semiotic systems, rituals, fashions, etc. through their manifestations in particular terms of the series. Note that if, say, the term $Te_2 e_3 e_5$ appears in Ω, this does not necessarily mean that the term $Te_2 e_3$ (the image of the material background in e_2 from the position of e_3) is also present. $Te_2 e_3 e_5$ may have been imagined by e_6, who constructed $Te_2 e_3 e_5$ and performed the transformation $Te_2 e_3 e_5 e_6 \rightarrow Te_2 e_3 e_5$.

If some personae believe in demons and "know" the demons' point of view on some matters, the investigator can represent this sort of reality by a symbolic series via attaching a label to each demon and including him in the series. If the investigator believes in demons, these personae will enter the series beginning with the second term, $\sum_i Te_i$.

(Evidently, the bodies of the demons may be present in T.) If the investigator does not believe in demons, these personae will appear only in the higher terms, and the extreme right index e_i will never be the label of a demon. In the same way, Othello and Tom Sawyer can be included in a social organism, as well as personae who, although already dead, are still "acting." Taking the elements as functions of time, history and planning can be introduced into the system. For instance, if e_7 is planning a material background T, this means that he is working out some Te_7, and the realization of the project will be a special degenerate case of reflexive control, namely, the transformation $Te_7 \rightarrow T$. Evidently all forms of mental planning can be regarded as a special type of reflexive control.

A most interesting manifestation of reflexive structures can be found in literature. Apparently, a reflexive analysis of literary works will enable us to discover features of reflexive structures in the social organism. It may also become a tool of philological analysis.

Collectives can be characterized by different degrees of satiation of reflexions corresponding to the different terms of the series. In the simplest mathematical models, only the presence or absence of particular reflexions can be fixated. This allows the determination of reflexively closed clusters of individuals, that is, those that have few or no images of personae belonging to other sets. Thus, the social organism can be partitioned into large components.

Personae, Positions, Roles, and Gitiks

We deem important the distinction between the concept of persona and that of role. A persona is an abstraction generated in some manner by identifying an individual as an event in space and taking him as a unit of observation. We label this individual and attribute an inner world to him. But an individual as an ongoing phenomenon is not necessarily an indivisible unit. In different social contexts and even in different situations, he may form different images, generated by different operators of awareness. In that case, the individual essentially splits and appears in quite different garbs. Therefore we must introduce a number of labels under which he will figure in different functionings of the system. A number of different positions can be "mounted" within the body of a single subject. These positions can exist independently as social phenomena. They may even be in conflict with each other. We cannot say that the persona "chose one or another position." The positions "parasitize" him. The persona does not possess a higher principle governing the interrelations of positions. Only external influences force him to take one or another position. Thus, positional boundaries do not lie between separate individuals. They lie in their inner worlds, separating one position from another by an unbridgeable abyss.

The notion of "role" has assumed an important meaning in contemporary sociology and psychology. It serves to separate some canonical social positions from the concrete person who occupies them. This serves, in turn, the process of identifying different structures in the social organism. The same person can "play different roles" in his family, in his work group, in his informal group, and so on. Evidently this notion stems from superimposing upon the social process the scheme of theatrical drama, where action is programmed by a scenario. In this case, normative interrelations (natural or legal) are the analogue of the scenario.

In spite of the effectiveness of the role concept, it may lead to severe confusion as a consequence of misuse. One application is that of determining the apportioning of an individual in the functional structure of the social organism. For example, an individual may be the head of a family, a rank-and-file member of a work group, and a scapegoat of an informal group. Another application brings out the artificially constructed internal spiritual visage. At other times, to play a role is to perform reflexive control. In still other situations, the role may be externally imposed, for instance the role of a prisoner. In this role, the persona is obliged, among other things, to address the guard in a prescribed way. The role becomes an adaptation to the environment: The prisoner's behavior communicates to the guard the absence of grounds for imposing a punishment—a borderline case of reflexive control.

In both applications of the role concept, it is tacitly assumed that it is possible for the individual to change roles voluntarily. If we now extend traditional phenomenology, based on the classification of various types of behavior, so as to include, as fully qualified elements, also the inner worlds in the process of gaining awareness, the role concept turns out to be too weak. Another conceptual approach is needed.

To take an example, the believer does not play the role of a believer (if we ignore some subtle aspects of ritual). He cannot abandon his state as a believer as long as the presence of faith is associated with a distinct "screen of consciousness" (cf., Chapter 1). God is an element of his inner world, essentially irremovable by the process of cognition. God is an organic component of the process. In some cases, a believer can play the role of an unbeliever, but he cannot become an unbeliever.

Therefore, when we pass from the analysis of networks of social structures to the objective study of the mental world as an element of the social organism in its own right, we need a new notion to express those aspects of the individual that are invariant with respect to the process of cognition, those that are essentially natural for him. The "screen of consciousness" is an example of such an aspect or else the presence of several independent positions, each with a corresponding screen of consciousness.

We call this "naturalness" from which the persona cannot escape independently and which determines the structure of his inner world (and through it his behavior) a *gitik*. This notion can be used in a wider or narrower sense, but always as an antipode of the artificial or the self-regulating aspect.

Reflexive Currency

Recall the chain "X thinks that Y thinks that X thinks . . ." examined in Chapter 2. For "thinks" we can substitute any of the following: knows, does not know, assumes, does not assume, is informed, is not informed. These phrases suggest a direction in the approach to the other's inner world, in some cases to one's own, as in "I know that I know that I know." Alternatives are also possible: "X knows that Y does not know that X knows."

The possibility of forming such chains speaks for the reflexive nature of the phrases. They arise in natural language as denoting processes associated with reflexive phenomenology. They are confined to only certain types of predicates; for instance, phrases like "is able" cannot be incorporated in an analogous chain. Clearly temporal nuances, present in natural language can also be registered, as in "X knows that Y knew that X will know."

The above phrases register the act of "filling the inner world of personae with information." Awareness of incompleteness also plays the part of a special sort of completeness. In natural language there are more refined means of registering reflexive completeness, for instance, "X is convinced that Y is convinced that X is convinced." More is registered than the state of being informed; "convinced" expresses a distinct quality of informedness.

The rules governing the formation of such chains should be of interest primarily to linguists. We are interested in the fact that all these chains are associated with information. They fit fully in the framework of our apparatus since they reflext in natural language the same "reality" for which we constructed our artificial language. In natural language, however, other kinds of chains can be built, like "X appreciates that Y appreciates that X appreciates . . ." Since these do not refer to information, we see that registration of values obeys the same regularities as that of being informed (cf., the passage on p. 51). Roughly speaking, if the other's information is a component of my information, then also, the other's values are a component of my values.

We shall present an illustrative model, developed jointly with P. V. Baranov and V. E. Lepsky, which describes the formation of values in reflexive "players" (Lefebvre, Baranov, Lepsky, 1969). Consider a person as a member of a group. Other members' values influence his. Others' pain is in some measure his pain. Of course, the coefficients of influence are individualized. In some individuals they are negative, which means that the pain of others is transformed into the persona's pleasure.

A kind of "external currency" is transformed into a kind of "internal currency" and so regulates activity. When we analyze so-called "irrational instances of social behavior," we encounter phenomena that must be explained by internal currency. In some cases, the adoption of an official currency depreciates a person in his own estimation, that is, devalues his internal currency. In other cases, the amount of internal currency depends on the models of other personae in the person's environment. In some cases, hurting others increases one's internal currency; in other cases it diminishes it. Sometimes a person can convert the external currency received by others into the others' internal currency, and his own internal currency will depend on the internal currency of others.

If we assume that individual currencies are objectively comparable, we can introduce the notion of the internal currency of groups, perhaps of society. In this sense every action and event has a "price" depending on how it changes the total currency potential. In this connection, an important ethical problem arises, that of choosing specific coefficients to be attached to the internal currency of each individual in calculating the total "sum." The very posing of the problem is evidently determined by the ethical position of the investigator (Rapoport, 1964).

In what follows, we offer the simplest approach to the problem of passing from external currency to internal. The essential task is to choose potentially measurable parameters in terms of which to express mutually reflected values. Let player X get payoff A and his partner payoff B. (These payoffs are determined by external, that is, "official" currency.) The way the payoffs are obtained is immaterial. We introduce two magnitudes, α and β. The parameter α characterizes X's attitude toward himself; β his attitude toward the partner (cf., Rapoport, 1956). We denote the internal currency of this player by

$$H_1^{(X)} = A + A\alpha + B\beta. \tag{13}$$

Let Y be characterized by the same parameters. Analogously, his internal currency will be defined by

$$H_1^{(Y)} = B + B\alpha + A\beta. \tag{14}$$

It is easy to see that α is the "amplifying coefficient" of the payoff. The coefficient β determines X's relation to Y. If X is indifferent to Y's joys and sorrows, $\beta = O$. If X is dissolved, so to say, in Y, lives by the latter's hopes and optimizes his gains, for instance, at cost to himself, β is positive and exceeds α. If X is hostile toward Y, that is, if Y's payoffs "hurt" X, $\beta < O$. In that case, if $B < O$, $B\beta > O$, which corresponds to obtaining additional payoff from Y's losses (Rapoport, 1956).

Let now X and Y become aware of their own internal currency and of that of their respective opponents. Each has somehow performed a calculation according to formulas (13) and (14). Of course, in reality no calculations take place. Simply for want of other methods of determining utilities, we had to use such crude intuitive tools.

Supposing that X reflects his opponent's utilities, he attributes coefficients α and β to him, of course, unconsciously. These are simply some objective characteristics of his reflexion. Assume that the internal currency obtained above is modified in the same way as the official currency, with which the process began:

$$H_2^{(X)} = H_1^{(X)} + H_1^{(X)} \alpha + H_1^{(Y)} \beta \ ;$$

$$H_2^{(Y)} = H_1^{(Y)} + H_1^{(Y)} \alpha + H_1^{(X)} \beta .$$

By iteration,

$$H_n^{(X)} = H_{n-1}^{(X)} + H_{n-1}^{(X)} \alpha + H_{n-1}^{(Y)} \beta; \qquad (15)$$

$$H_n^{(Y)} = H_{n-1}^{(Y)} + H_{n-1}^{(Y)} \alpha + H_{n-1}^{(X)} \beta. \qquad (16)$$

This iterative process, generating internal currency resembles the development of the reflexive polynomial $\Omega = T(1 + x + y)^n$. The essential difference is in that each act of awareness in principle maintains a structure of awareness, whereas in the development of internal currency, the history appears as a "valuation" rather than a cognitive structure.

It is interesting to examine the case when the sequence of currencies generated by iteration converges to some value. In seeking a limiting evaluation, we avoid the necessity of examining a vast number of variants of finite awareness. We obtain a certain operator that produces the evaluation of internal currency depending only on the magnitudes A and B and the parameters α and β. Define $H_o^{(X)} = A$, $H_o^{(Y)} = B$.

To express $H_n^{(X)}$ in terms of A, B, α, and β, we add termwise equations (15) and (16), then subtract (16) from (15). We have

$$H_n^{(X)} + H_n^{(Y)} = (H_{n-1}^{(X)} + H_{n-1}^{(Y)}) + (H_{n-1}^{(X)} + H_{n-1}^{(Y)} \alpha +$$

$$H_{n-1}^{(X)} + H_{n-1}^{(Y)}) \beta$$

$$= (H_{n-1}^{(X)} + H_{n-1}^{(Y)}) (1 + \alpha + \beta) \qquad (17)$$

$$= (A + B) (1 + \alpha + \beta)^n$$

$$H_n^{(X)} - H_n^{(Y)} = (H_{n-1}^{(X)} - H_{n-1}^{(Y)}) + (H_{n-1}^{(X)} - H_{n-1}^{(Y)})\alpha$$

$$+ (H_{n-1}^{(Y)} - H_{n-1}^{(X)})\beta$$

$$= (H_{n-1}^{(X)} - H_{n-1}^{(Y)}) (1 + \alpha - \beta)$$

$$= (A - B) (1 + \alpha - \beta)^n. \tag{18}$$

So far we have assumed that α and β do not depend on the rank of reflexion. We may now introduce a "discount factor," whereby the parameters become inversely proportional to the order of reflexion:[1][2]

$$\alpha = \frac{\alpha_o}{n}, \; \beta = \frac{\beta_o}{n}.$$

Letting n go to infinity, we obtain as limiting values

$$H^{(X)} + H^{(Y)} = (A + B)\exp(\alpha_o + \beta_o) \tag{19}$$

$$H^{(X)} - H^{(Y)} = (A - B)\exp(\alpha_o - \beta_o) \tag{20}$$

Hence,

$$H^{(X)} = \tfrac{1}{2}(A + B)\exp(\alpha_o + \beta_o) + \tfrac{1}{2}(A - B)\exp(\alpha_o - \beta_o).$$

Rearranging and using hyperbolic functions, we have,

$$H^{(X)} = (A \cosh \beta_o + B \sinh \beta_o) \exp \alpha_o, \tag{21}$$

as the limiting value sought. The parameter β_o can be interpreted as the "angle" between the players.

It is easy to see that in passing from external to internal currency, β_o plays the more important role, since α_o reflects only the "scale" of internal currency in the matrix of these currencies. The ratio of the elements of the matrix, on the other hand, is determined by β_0 (assuming, of course, that α_0 and β_0 are not functions of A and B).

It is possible to find test games specifically designed for determining β_0. Without loss of generality, suppose that the maximal payoff in official currency is one unit. In our test, X chooses an arbitrary point on the circle $x^2 + y^2 = 1$ (cf., Figure 7.1). Then his own official payoff will be denoted by

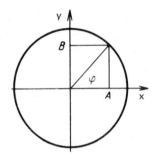

Figure 7.1

$\cos(\varphi)$. Correspondingly, the other's payoff will be denoted by $\sin(\varphi)$, so that $A = \cos(\varphi)$, $B = \sin(\varphi)$. We suppose that the player chooses φ to maximize his own internal utility, which makes it possible to determine β_0. Elementary analysis shows that for any real β_0, the optimizing value of φ satisfies the inequality $-\pi/4 \leqslant \varphi = \pi/4$.

Note that in this model the subject is not assumed to take into account the effect of his choice on the value of β_0, which will be subsequently used by the other player. The point is that in choosing egotistically, X may impair Y's "good will." Therefore X's actual decisions depend eventually on how "controls" the magnitude of β_0, associated with the other player.

The scheme can be generalized to the case where an arbitrary number of personae interact, the ratio parameters being arbitrary real numbers. Let m be the number of personae and $W_0 = (a_{ij})$, $i,j = 1, \cdots m$ the matrix of ratios. We obtain obvious generalizations of (13) and (14), namely,

$$H_n^{(1)} = H_{n-1}^{(1)} + \sum_{j=1}^{m} H_{n-1}^{(j)} a_{1j} \frac{}{n},$$

$$\cdot \cdot \cdot \cdot \cdot \cdot \cdot \cdot \cdot \cdot \cdot \cdot \cdot \cdot \cdot \cdot \cdot \qquad (22)$$

$$H_n^{(m)} = H_{n-1}^{(m)} + \sum_{j=1}^{m} H_{n-1}^{(j)} a_{mj} \frac{}{n}.$$

Writing the equations in matrix form, we have

$$\begin{pmatrix} H_n^{(1)} \\ \cdot \\ \cdot \\ \cdot \\ \cdot \\ H_n^{(m)} \end{pmatrix} = \begin{pmatrix} H_{n-1}^{(1)} \\ \cdot \\ \cdot \\ \cdot \\ \cdot \\ H_{n-1}^{(m)} \end{pmatrix} + \frac{W_0}{n} \begin{pmatrix} H_{n-1}^{(1)} \\ \cdot \\ \cdot \\ \cdot \\ \cdot \\ H_{n-1}^{(m)} \end{pmatrix} = (I + \frac{W_0}{n}) \begin{pmatrix} H_{n-1}^{(1)} \\ \cdot \\ \cdot \\ \cdot \\ \cdot \\ H_{n-1}^{(m)} \end{pmatrix} \qquad (23)$$

Where I is the identity matrix. Applying the recursive relations (23), we have

$$\begin{pmatrix} H_n^{(1)} \\ \cdot \\ \cdot \\ \cdot \\ \cdot \\ H_n^{(m)} \end{pmatrix} = (I + \frac{W_0}{n})^n \begin{pmatrix} H_0^{(1)} \\ \cdot \\ \cdot \\ \cdot \\ \cdot \\ H_0^{(m)} \end{pmatrix}$$

or, in abridged form,

$$H_n = (I + \frac{W_0}{n})^n H_0.$$

As n approaches infinity, we obtain in the limit

$$H = \exp(W_o) H_o.$$

The internal currencies of each individual in the population can be calculated from the matrix of relations and the column of payments. The purely illustrative function of this model is again emphasized.[13]

The Origin of Reflexion and Language

The presence of reflexive connections essentially distinguishes the human collective from other types. One of the principal mechanisms of functional socialization in a human collective is the replication of reasoning. This makes it possible for the collective to function during long stretches of time without direct informational contacts among the members and also to maintain its integrity even against considerable spatial and temporal discontinuities. Replicated reasoning appears as a special tool for coordinating and synchronizing the activities of the individual members. Besides, the streams of information are shortened inasmuch as their function is not so much that of transmitting data as that of communicating replicating activity. The collective can be regarded as fully formed only when all the members are endowed with means of replicating the decision-procedures of the other members. We shall examine an illustrative model of a primitive collective and will attempt to construct mechanisms giving rise to simplest forms of reflexion. First, we examine such a mechanism with respect to reflexion of the "zero-th" order. Here an individual himself is reflected in his own "map," but the map is not reflected in itself.

We introduce a distinction between a rank-and-file member and a leader. A leader performs the function of establishing the situational structures of the collective. This is his only function. Each member can choose among different working procedures, w_1, w_2, ... The procedures are not inherently connected. They are arranged into sequences only by the leader's signals.

All the members of the collective operate on reality. The leader operates on a distinct feature of reality, namely, the collective. He is thrust out of the collective and stands over it. He can perform his function only if he "assimilates" this reality, reflects it on a special map, and then realizes it. The map must reflect the individual rank-and-file members, objects assimilated by them, and the phases of the procedure performed by them. Thus we have two bases in the collective:

1. The working procedures performed by the rank-and-file members.

2. A special work operation related to the collective, performed by the leader with the aid of a special semiotic tool, namely, the map.

Evidently, we can establish the origin of the collective only when the aggregate is transformed into a reflexive system, that is, when semiotic tools for planning the activity of the collective as a unit make their appearance.

Let us now introduce limits on the number of rank-and-file members when the scope of required work remains constant. In a small collective, the member who is the leader must perform rank-and-file functions along with those of the leader. In many problems, the leader must reflect himself on his map as a material surrogate along with the rank-and-file members, for instance in the problem of distributing products.

Now a different procedure is started. Both bases are combined in the leader, the working and the organizing activity (cf., Figure 7.2a). For the first time, individual activity becomes internally organized. The mechanism, which at first acted on the scale of the collective, becomes an individual activity. The leader is transformed into a self-reflexive system.

The signaling system controlling the collective must first become an individual activity of the leader. But as long as there are no spatial discontinuities, which this activity was supposed to overcome, the signals disappear, and a direct connection is established between the map and the working

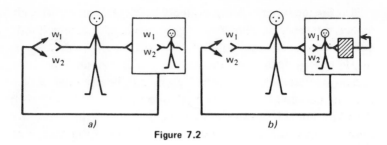

Figure 7.2

procedures. It seems that the combination of the two different activities as a result of individuals becoming reflected in their own maps amounts to the origin of individual reflexion.

The "ego" originates as an external material surrogate of the leader. At first, the loss of this material surrogate is the loss of reflexion. Only later, being reflected by the physiological apparatus, the surrogate enters the "head." Individual consciousness cannot originate "in the head." To explain its origin, it is necessary to examine the structure of collective activity and the evolution of semiotic tools. The problems related to the origin of man and of primitive society are in the first instance semiotic problems.

Reflexion of zero-th order arises in the leader. However, this too has the property of recurrence. Under certain conditions the map and the activity on it can be reflected on that very map. In this way, a special form of planning activity arises, which already amounts to individual intellectual activity (cf., Figure 7.2b).

When replications of the members' own intellectual activity appear in a collective, entirely new possibilities are opened up. Replication of one's own intellectual activity makes it possible to replicate the activity of other members without reconstructing the semiotic means of such replication. As the rank-and-file members acquire the means of replication, they need not continually receive real signals from the leader. Put in a situation where direct contact with the leader is not possible, they replicate his reasoning, work out corresponding decisions, the replicate the "translation of the decision addressed to themselves and act accordingly."

("This is what father would have done!") However, the possession of these mechanisms already contains the possibility of reflexive conflicts and the appearance of normative institutions (religions, ideologies, etc.).

Another possible scheme of the origin of individual reflexion can be sketched. As in the preceding scheme, consider the situation where semiotic tools for representing the environment have already appeared but are still "external" with respect to the acting subject. Internalization, that is, the transformation of external acts into "psychic functioning" has not yet appeared in the philogeny of man (Vygotsky, 1934; Galperin, 1966; Leontiev, 1965).

The semiotic tools that have assumed the role of surrogates of real objects enabled a being (whose behavior had been predetermined by a "receptive field," that is, the field of perceiving objects by the senses) to pass to a particular perception of these objects. For an image of a "river" to appear, one needs a rope, which helps to conceptualize the river. It is not the image of the river that produces the analogy "river—rope." It is the use of a rope in a definite familiar function with respect to a sensually unperceptible whole that serves to compensate for this sensual imperceptibility. The rope organizes different particular images relating to the river and arranges them in a definite sequence. Motion along the rope begins to govern the transformation of images.

The entire further intellectual evolution of "social man" was directed toward the creation of means of representing ever wider areas of reality that could not be perceived by the senses. The solar system cannot be perceived as a whole. A special model was needed, and it was this model that helped organize both social experience and social memory.

Let us return to the problem of the origin of reflexion. The ego cannot be perceived by the senses. Just for this reason, the ego, like the river or the solar system must first originate outside.

Consider the communication between two primitive personae who have external semiotic tools for representing the world but no language. They communicate on a "map." X perceives Y but does not perceive himself. He registers Y's existence on his model, say with a pebble. Y does likewise, perceiving X but not himself. He registers X's existence by another pebble. The map, however, belongs to both and combines them into a single system. Whereas each persona separately had only an image of the other, together they have two images. Then each individually acquires two images, one of himself, one of his partner (cf., Figure 7.3). And so

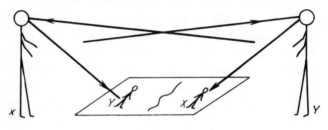

Figure 7.3

we see that it is possible to construct a model of reflexion originating in cooperative activity, namely, in communication through a semiotic map. Of course, we have offered only a sketch of a model. We have not touched on the question how the self is identified. But the model serves to approach the problem of the origin of language in a new way.

A characteristic difficulty of this problem relates to the impossibility of deducing a language from the signaling systems of animals. A signal set by an animal is directed at "plugging in" some definite action. It lacks the function of denoting objects or events. Language signs, on the other hand, are perceived by us as related in considerable degree to the world of things. In fact, even actions are registered as special kinds of things. There have been numerous attempts to overcome this difficulty and to deduce a language from a system of signalization. In our opinion, this approach is without prospects.

We return to our scheme of communication through a model. Imagine this model in a specific stationary setting. In order to communicate, we must occupy a definite location and assume a definite "working" position. Imagine now that this setting has to be moved in space.[14] To do this, one must disassemble the model and then assemble it in a new location. This, in turn, necessitates labeling the disassembled parts. The disassembled device can be regarded as a linear sequence of labeled components of a map, and this sequence is already essentially a language. Language is a stream of disassembled elements. In the phylogenic process, some "sound" is put into correspondence to each element of the disassembled system. A sound language is essentially a code that registers not elements of the real world but rather elements of a disassembled map and a labeling. In phylogenesis, the map, its disassembly, and reassembly are internalized. An external technical device is no longer necessary for communicating. The act of speech appears as a means of transmitting labeled components of the disassembled model belonging to the speaker. The process of understanding appears as that of assembling a configuration on the map belonging to the hearer.

We emphasize the most essential feature of this scheme. Elements of language have no analogues in the real world. Their analogues are the elements of the map, which, as a whole, has a correspondence to reality.

In our model, the communicating personae are represented without any linguistic attributes. In presenting this model as a primary means of communication, we pose anew the problem of communicating with dolphins.[15] To do this, we must create special means of indication that would enable the dolphin (taking into account its receptive potentialities) to perceive both itself and the experimenter as elements of the external world. Communication must become a manipulation of the model by both. For instance, if the experimenter wants to meet the dolphin in a given location of the pool, he must move the representation of himself in the model, then the representation of the dolphin to that location. If an experiment of this sort succeeds, it will serve as evidence that two very different cultures have come into contact.

Some researchers (in the Soviet Union and in the United States) assume that the communication system of dolphins may be similar to television broadcasting but created by sound waves instead of electromagnetic waves. The dolphins' vocal picture of the world is apparently more like the human visual picture than human vocal picture. One can say that dolphins see by "means of their ears." One dolphin can send a picture of reality to another dolphin.

If this hypothesis is true, a consequence is that a dolphin can have a picture of itself in its inner world. Let us suppose that dolphin X is sending to dolphin Y a "TV-picture" of reality. Since the body of dolphin Y is a part of this reality, dolphin Y, who has the picture of reality from dolphin X, should find itself in this picture. Thus, dolphin X is a peculiar mirror for dolphin Y.

If we assume that dolphins can resend the pictures, the structure of· their inner world can be expressed with complicated reflexive polynomials. Suppose that dolphin Z is sending some picture to dolphin X, and that dolphin X is resending this picture to dolphin Y.

Dolphin Z would be expressed by the following polynomial:

$$\Omega_1 = T + Tz;$$

dolphin X:

$$\Omega_2 = T + (T + Tz)x;$$

dolphin Y:

$$\Omega_3 = T + [T + (T + Tz)x]y;$$

If we accept this hypothesis, we see a structure very similar to the human reflexive system with the enormous difference that the dolphin's reflexive system does not depend on things —models nor on any activity connected with them (cf., the example with the rope, p. 157). It is a completely biological version of "civilization." To human language corresponds "TV-scanning" (pictures transformed into currents of signs).

The ability to have several pictures from different points of view allows each dolphin to receive a large amount of information. This capacity, as opposed to the elements of human culture, is hereditary. It is both an advantage and a weakness: "The dolphins' culture" is closed in the area of direct perception. It can develop only with biological evolution.

The models used by primitive man to reflect reality were outside of his head. (There were only pictures of those models inside his head.) Their nonbiological nature let them develop intensively and reflect the reality which could not be perceived.

Using the reflexive criteria we are obligated to consider the dolphins' system as a special civilization, developed on a completely different basis. This civilization does not have industry or universities, but it has reflexive structures.

We may try to come in contact with dolphins by using external models; however, it may be more efficient to include ourselves into the dolphins' communication system. (Today this problem seems immensely complicated.)

All of this is based on the hypothesis that dolphins can exchange vocal pictures. Only if this is true, it seems, does everything above become practically interesting. However, this example illustrates very well the idea of the autonomy of reflexive structures from concrete systems. Perhaps the concept of reflexive structures is as basic as, for example, the concept of feedback.

Chapter 8

CONFIGURATORS AND

POLYNOMIALS

In all existing scientific disciplines there are traditional methods of classification that manifest themselves as a concretized norm of human activity. We attach a specific label to a real object, thus bringing out those of its aspects that we need in order to solve the problems posed in a given science. Tradition plays an enormous part in this process. Many classifications arose in consequence of several centuries of practice in solving concrete problems. They became universally adopted and were canonized. In logical analysis it is very difficult to separate these classifications from the objects, to realize that they are only special tools of human cognition required in the solution of traditional problems. For instance, as a consequence of many centuries of medical practice, the human organism appears as a system of organs, e.g., brain, kidneys, liver, etc. From childhood on, we learn this classification, and it is difficult for us to admit that if medical practice developed in some other way, the partioning of the human organism into canonical elements would have been different; that is, the human organism would be regarded as consisting of different "organs."

New problems generate new classifications. We must not think that nontraditional systemic conceptions are "unreal" and can be ultimately reduced to traditional ones. They are simply different, because they arise in connection with attempts to solve different sorts of problems.

The Configurator

Some problems can be solved only if several mutually connected systems and conceptions are utilized. In each conception, the whole is partitioned into different elements. It is as if the object were projected upon a number of different screens, each showing a different partitioning and so generating a different structure. The screens are mutually connected, so that the investigator can relate the different pictures without recourse to the object itself. A device of this sort, one that synthesizes different systemic conceptions will be called a *configurator* (Lefebvre, 1962; 1965b; Schedrovitsky, 1971; Blauberg, Sadovsky, Yudin, 1969).

Evidently, configurators can be identified as special devices in all spheres of human knowledge. They are manifested more distinctly in technical disciplines. For instance, in electronics a "system" of systemic conceptions is used: the block diagram, the functional diagram, and the assembly scheme, all pertaining to the same device. The block diagram can be defined in terms of the technical units produced in industry and accordingly the device is partitioned into these units. The functional diagram presupposes an entirely different partition. It must explain the functioning of the device. In it the functioning units are brought out, which may have no spatially localized analogues. Pieces of equipment may have different block schemes and the same functioning scheme and vice versa. Finally, the assembly scheme partitions the object according to the geometrical space within which the assembly must be confined.

Knowledge of the device comes only through a synthesis of the various partitions. It is impossible to answer a seemingly simple question, namely, what are the elements of which the device consists, without indicating the appropriate schematic conception. The configurational conception of an object is widely used in descriptive geometry. Any diagram of a part in three projections is the result of using cartesian coordinates—an example of a geometric configurator.

Systemic Conceptions of an Object in the Investigator's Reflexion

The investigator can recognize systemic conceptions as distinct stereotypes, provided he has appropriate means for registering his means of systemic conception. In addition, the investigator needs a special tool for representing the object (Schedrovitsky, 1966) in order to integrate mentally the different conceptions. He must be able to say, "These are different representations of the same thing." This idea of "the same thing" must be fixated in a particular way.

The systemic conception and the object in the investigator's reflexion can be represented as in Figure 8. The squares on the left are different representations, generally speaking, of different objects. They become different projections of a simple object (in the inner world of the investigator) as they

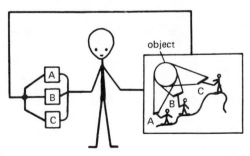

Figure 8

are connected to the reflexive image, placed in the manikin's left hand. The figure shows the path along which the investigator mentally passes from one position to the other. This path represents the connection between the two positions. The properties and qualities of objects recognized by the investigator are partitioned in his inner world into two classes. Some he relates to the object, and they appear to him as attributes characterizing the object as such; others appear as being generated by the frames, A, B, C, through which he sees the object. These characterize the various positions, which we denote by X_1, X_2, and X_3. If we denote the manikin's external position by Y, the whole situation, that is, the configurator, can be represented by the reflexive polynomial

$$(T + Tx_1 + Tx_2 + Tx_3)y.$$

As an example, let Tx_1 be a schematization of the object in terms of cybernetics, Tx_2 in terms of physics. There are four possible cases:

$$\Omega_1 = T + Tx_1 + Tx_2$$

$$\Omega_2 = (T + Tx_1 + Tx_2)x_2$$

$$\Omega_3 = (T + Tx_1 + Tx_2)x_1$$

$$\Omega_4 = (T + Tx_1 + Tx_2)x_3$$

In the first case, the investigator does not have a holistic picture. He is not aware of his means. The world appears to him in two aspects, on the one hand as a vast cybernetic machine, on the other as reality subjected only to physical laws. There is no connection between the two pictures. In the second case, the situation is viewed from the point of view of physics, that is, reduced to physical models. In the third case, the picture is reduced to a cybernetic model. The fourth case characterizes scientific creativity, which generates a new position. Using the analogy of reflexive games, we regard this case as a construction of a new player, who is aware of the pictures presented to previously constructed players.[16]

We may suppose that scientific knowledge can be schematized as a reflexive polynomial in which the various investigative positions correspond to different personae. In this sense, the plugging in to a "scientific organism" amounts to an investigation of a reflexive object. Learning will appear as an acquisition of positions, and creative activity as an attack on the whole structure: the liquidation of some personae, the addition of others, the construction of juxtaposed and competing investigative positions. The role of the "object as such" is assumed by T inside the parenthesis. However, from the position of an external observer, say X, it is also a particular systemic conception. The latter has an objective "privilege." The other systemic conceptions are recognized by the investigator as deducible from his.

For instance, astronomers recognize two different frameworks. In one, the sun and planets are conceived as the heliocentric system; in the other, they appear as attached fixed to the heavenly sphere. Hardware analogues of these frameworks are the tellurion and the planetarium respectively. However, one of these conceptions, represented by the tellurion, is regarded as the "real," while the other, represented by the planetarium, is considered to be reducible to the former and used only for convenience. Denoting the planetarium as x_1 and the tellurion as x_2, the interdependence of the two positions can be expressed as $(T + Tx_1)x_2$.

In recent times, physics has assumed the role of the tellurion. Many biologists, cyberneticians, and physicists are convinced that they can acquire genuine exhaustive knowledge of their fields if they can reduce all regularities to physical laws. The situation has a historical explanation. Physics was already quite developed when biology was not yet a unified science and there was no conception of a complex system. When physicists were creating cosmological models, they did not worry about how their world can be "peopled," first with biological entities, then with reason, developing civilizations and, perhaps, even with more complex objects. The matter here concerns not the well-known Second Law of Thermodynamics, which, for some reason, is regarded as the archenemy of biological entities. The matter concerns the specifics of physical models. They are simply not suited for investigations of this sort.

Chapter 9

REFLEXION AND COSMOLOGY

From the point of view of natural philosophy, one of the most remarkable properties of the universe is the presence in it of entities that are able to construct models of it. We are the reflexive systems of the universe. We are a sort of "retina" upon which the universe contemplates itself. The universe as a whole is representable in the form

$$\Omega = T + Tx,$$

where T is the material world and Tx its image, in some mysterious way contained in it. From the purely materialistic point of view, we must assume that Tx is reducible to T:

$$T \supset Tx.$$

Any purely mentalistic approach is described by the opposite relation:

$$Tx \supset T,$$

where the reality T is deducible from its image Tx.

Besides these, two dualistic approaches suggest themselves. The first is "neutral dualism," describable by the two relations

$$T \not\supset Tx$$

$$Tx \not\supset T.$$

The other is "paradoxical dualism" (Lefebvre, 1970). It requires simultaneous validity of

$$T \supset Tx$$

$$Tx \supset T.$$

One possible model that realizes the scheme of paradoxical dualism will be discussed in the next chapter.

If we admit that we are a part of the universe, we must regard the universe itself as a reflexive system. This incontrovertible conclusion is outside the framework of contemporary natural science. Traditionally, it was considered only in philosophy. Nevertheless, this "fact" is no less significant than the "fact" that space and time exist. Yet the path of development of our science has been such that we cannot even pose any clear-cut problems related to the universe as a whole regarded as a reflexive system.

What path shall we follow then? The simplest is that of accepting neutral dualism, since along that path the question how "spiritual essence" is connected to matter requires no answer. Other approaches require constructive explanations of how mind and matter are related or else lead to the conclusion that the question has no answer or that the problem is not properly put.

Obviously, we cannot solve the problem at this time. In this chapter only some "mock-ups" of cosmological models will be offered, not actual models. These mock-ups will serve as illustrations of how a theory must look if it is to show that the world is not confined to the framework of physical conceptions. We shall show that a model based on simple topological or mechanical foundations can force us to admit the existence of entities which from the point of view of natural science cannot be regarded as real. The entities can be interpreted in different ways. One possible interdependence is in terms of a mental phenomenology.

A Two-Faced Cosmology

In recent decades, a new cosmology has been coming into being, juxtaposed to the physical. Its task is to include biological reality into the world picture, as a sort of "norm," natural and indispensable. The origin of this new cosmology ought to be linked in the first instance with the works of M. L. Tsetlin (1973), E. F. Moore, (1964), W. R. Ashby (1962), and L. Löfgren (1958). We will examine some possible models and principles of their construction in which living organisms and civilizations on the one hand and the phenomena of the physical picture on the other appear as different manifestations of a simple construct. In building physical pictures, in particular cosmological ones, it is taken for granted that "order" and "chaos" are absolute characteristics, independent of the organizing principle governing the observer and his instruments of cognition. We will drop this assumption and will show that it is possible to build a model that is a symbiosis of two self-organizing systems realized on the same substrate. Whether events are characterized by the observer as organized or random will depend on the "branch" of organization that characterizes him and his instrument (Lefebvre, 1967; 1969c).

We illustrate this idea by an example encountered in many popular books on psychology. The sketch shown in Figure 9.1 represents either a human profile or a mouse. We can see this drawing in two ways, and what we see depends on how we schematize it. Let the reader now imagine that the mouse and the profile each have a life of their own. Let them (not the external observer) look at themselves, feel their "wholeness," and try to change the configuration of their parts. For instance, the mouse wiggles its tail and thereby wrinkles the skin on the profile's neck. In order for each to exist and to maintain its identity (as a mouse or as a profile), each must fulfill certain obligations toward the other.

Figure 9.1

Next, assume that one of them can change in a way that preserves its essential features but destroys the other. The basic idea can be illustrated by a well known puzzle. Fifteen squares numbered 1 to 15 are placed on a 4 x 4 grid. The one empty square makes it possible to shift the squares to adjacent positions. Initially they are in random order. The task is to put them in consecutive order.

Imagine now that the squares are labeled on both sides by different numbers in haphazard correspondence. The game is played by two persons on the opposite sides of the grid. Each will perceive the actions of the other as chaotic, generally destructive of what appears to him as an ordered configuration. Suppose now neither player is allowed to frustrate the efforts of the other. By way of compromise, if some "local" ordering on one side destroys order on the other, the player on that side is permitted to bring order at another location. Someone observing one side will conclude that an increase of order in region C takes place at the cost of a decrease of order in region D and will interpret this finding as a transfer of "entropy" from C to D.

Here the entropic picture becomes a consequence of the observer's position. He establishes connections with the "metric" of a given surface but not the connections with the "antipodes." His aim is to get an adequate picture of a "one-sided" existence of the system visible to him.

In the framework of a two-faced cosmology, civilizations can be regarded as regions, where the degree of organization of a system on one side of a surface is significantly greater than that on the antipodal side and continues to increase.

In this connection, one-sided surfaces illustrated by Moebius strips are especially interesting (cf., Figure 9.2). On such a surface, configurations that appear to be antipodal are actually adjacent!

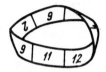

Figure 9.2

If we accept the hypothesis that physical space is a one-sided surface, then the fact that this space is a three-dimensional manifold immersed in a four-dimensional one implies the existence of a self-intersecting two-dimensional manifold (an "edge") as in the analogues represented by the Klein bottle or the Moebius strip. In other words, an impenetrable wall must be "stretched" over physical space. Let this wall reflect light. If also this hypothesis is accepted, it appears that a huge mirror is stretched in space in which the system reflects itself.

The fact that the wall is essentially two-dimensional is important. We speak here not of an abstract two-dimensionality, where we ignore the thickness of an object, but of a physical property, a consequence of the three-dimensionality of space. Thus, a "mysterious reality" appears in our construct, a two-dimensional surface. We have no idea what it is. (The reader must keep in mind that we are not engaged in a real theoretical investigation. We only "play" at constructing a theory. Our game, however, shows how an "unreal entity" can suddenly appear in a theory.)

We cannot speak of the physical status of two-dimensional things, since we have no idea of what such things might be. Our model becomes open-ended. The first steps into the unknown are always speculative. What if the partition turns out to be the "sensual retina" of mental substance?

We do not know how to proceed with the reasoning. Evidently, the models of natural science can only point to "suspicious" essences that may turn out to have no connection to mental phenomenology. Of course, in this case, we remain in the purely materialistic scheme of reasoning: $T \supset Tx$. We attempt to deduce the existence of Tx from T.

The Two-Faced Cosmology and Time's Arrow

Another line of speculation is suggested by the one-sided surafce model of the cosmos. Suppose the "degree of organization" of a system remains constant, that is, an increase of organization in one locality implies a decrease in another. Again we represent the universe by a Moebius strip partitioned as follows:

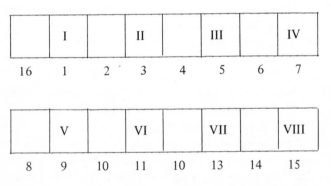

The lower squares are the "opposite sides" of the upper. The total degree of organization is assumed constant.

Let an observer be attached to each square denoted by a roman numeral. He records the state of the region where he

is and two adjoining regions. Further, each observer has discovered that in his "world" the Second Law of Thermodynamics is validated. That is, the degree of organization
in each of his regions decreases. This leads the observer in
square I to suppose that the entropy in any sufficiently large
region is increasing. But in view of the original assumption
that the sum of the entropies of each region and its antipode
remains constant, the degree of organization of region V is
increasing; consequently, its entropy is decreasing. Our observer is forced to conclude that "time flows in opposite
directions" in antipodal regions.

On the other hand, the observer in region I can communicate with the observer in region II via the square between
them, which they both observe. They find that for them time
flows in the same direction. Similarly, the observer at II can
communicate with the observer at III. Continuing, we find
that time flows in the same direction everywhere, contradict-
ing the previous conclusion.

The paradox can be resolved if we assume that the "rate
of time" relative to a given square decreases with distance
from it. At a sufficiently large distance, time appears to stand
still, and at still further distances, its direction is reversed. To
illustrate let us designate the time interval by

$$\Delta t = \cos (k\pi/n)^{-1}$$

where $n = N/2$, N being the (even) number of squares, and k
is the "distance" between successive squares. Then at $k = 0$,
$\Delta t = 1$. In our case, $n = 8$. Thus at $k = 4$, $\Delta t = (\cos \pi/2)^{-1} = \infty$. At $k = 8$, $\Delta t = -1$.

Thus, each region has a "horizon," where time "stands
still" relative to that region and beyond which it flows in the
opposite direction. In such a universe, the shift toward the
red in the spectra of distant nebulae is observed. Its cause,
however, is not the centrifugal flight of the galaxies but
rather the slowing down of time at distant objects. The
model resembles De Sitter's (A. S. Eddington, 1924) but

differs from the latter in that a one-sided surface replaces a sphere as the spatial manifold. The present model serves to identify in a natural manner spatially separated points and to relate time curvature to the degree of organization.

Chapter 10

SYSTEMS DRAWN ON SYSTEMS

We shall attempt to examine the possibilities suggested by the paradoxical-dualistic scheme of reasoning:

$$T \supset Tx$$

$$Tx \supset T.$$

Organism and Substance

When we speak of systems, we frequently assume the existence of a substance in which they are realized and which determine their existence. We encounter the first contradiction when we examine the simplest living organisms. Norbert Wiener used to say, "The identity of a body is more like the identity of a flame than that of a stone; it is the identity of a structure, not of a piece of matter." The organism as a whole is not determined by its "atoms." It is nevertheless no less real than a stone, composed of a fixed amount of matter.

The Organism as a Wave

There have been interesting attempts to model living organisms by automata with a cell-like structure. Each element of such an automaton can be in any of a finite number of states. A configuration of "active" states of its cells represents the organism. A moving organism can be represented as a kind of wave (Löfgren, 1958). Such automata reproduce certain features of living organisms and, moreover, can be viewed as explanations of several processes. Nevertheless, although we can separate the organisms from concrete "atoms," we still have to do with a substance upon which the organism moves like a wave. The substance is primary. The wave is secondary. Without a substance, there is no wave.

The Relation-Tissue Pattern

An author of a fantastic story placed some thousands of persons in a stadium. Each performed the function of a computer. Imagine that this computer with persons as components has worked for several years. During this time, the substance of the organisms has been replaced. They now consist of other atoms, but they remain the same persons. Now imagine that the computer "glides" over the substrate of human organisms. For instance, on succeeding days each person performs the function that was performed by his neighbor on the previous day. The structure of the computer does not change thereby. In this way, we have built a stable functioning structure that glides along another functioning structure which, in turn, glides over the material substrate. The substrate of the computer consists of the functioning systems of human organization; the substrate of the latter is the field of "atoms."

The human bodies are related to the field of atoms in one way and to the computer in another. With respect to the atoms, the bodies are a functioning system; with respect to the computer, the bodies are an inert substrate, the space in which the system exists. We shall call the relation between a functional scheme and the substrate "tissue-pattern." It is as if the functional scheme were "drawn" on the substrate. This pattern, however, is not analogous to that on a carpet. It is rather like a moving picture. Patterns may be superimposed on other patterns as when a moving picture is shown inside another moving picture. Here the substrate is the screen; the film is a pattern on the screen; the film within the film is a pattern on a pattern.

Closed Chains of Tissue-Pattern Relations

From the above examples, we see that the tissue-pattern relations can form chains, as indicated by arrows in Figure 10.1. The elements of this structure are not functionally equivalent. For instance, element 1 in Figure 10.1, symbolizing the field of atoms, functions only as tissue, that is, matter as such. It is not a pattern on some other "deeper" tissue. Having drawn this diagram, the author was seized by an irresistible desire to deprive element 1 of its privileged position. To do this, it is sufficient to close the chain, as in Figure 10.2, so that element 1 "becomes" a pattern. Now

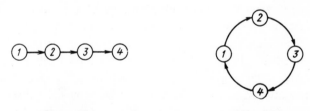

| Figure 10.1 | Figure 10.2 |

all the elements are functionally equivalent; each fulfills two roles. At once, the question arises whether closing the chain is not a mere exercise in formalism. Or can we think of a reasonable construct that would be functional and organized as a ring?

Closed Chains of Automata as
Patterns "Drawn" on Each Other

Let a field of cells be given as shown in Figure 10.3. Let each cell be in one of four states, a_1, b_1, c_1, d_1. We shall call the configuration of four elements, a_1, b_1, c_1, d_1, an "organism" filling our space. Suppose that each state is a self-reproducing system: a_1 is reproduced in the cell where b_1 was "located" in the preceding moment; b_1 is reproduced where c_1 had been, and so on. Finally, d_1 is reproduced where a_1 had been in the preceding moment. It is easy to see that the system a_1, b_1, c_1, d_1, left to itself, will rotate clockwise (cf., Figure 10.4). Here the cells are the tissue, the rotating states are the pattern.

Figure 10.3

Figure 10.4

Now imagine that each of the states a_1, b_1, c_1, d_1 can be in one of four other states, a_2, b_2, c_2, d_2. We construct another automaton and place it upon the moving automaton. The rules of representation of the states are the same as above. Now the system a_2, b_2, c_2, d_2 starts to rotate clockwise along the "tissue" represented by the automaton a_1, b_1, c_1, d_1. Relative to the paper to which the field of cells belongs, the automaton a_2, b_2, c_2, d_2 moves by skipping a cell each time. Now introduce another automaton, a_3, b_3, c_3, d_3. Relative to the paper, a_3, b_3, c_3, d_3 will be skipping two cells at a time, and a_4, b_4, c_4, d_4 will be skipping three. That is to say, a_4, b_4, c_4, d_4 will appear to be stationary relative to the paper. This is the automaton that we identify with the paper, that is, with the field of cells. Thus, a_1, b_1, c_1, d_1 are states that can be assumed by the automaton a_4, b_4, c_4, d_4.

It is interesting to note that an observer who registers a_4, b_4, c_4, d_4 as stationary will see a_3, b_3, c_3, d_3 rotating counter-clockwise. There is an analogous effect in moving pictures when the wheel of a vehicle appears to be rotating in the "wrong" direction.

The example illustrates the illusory character of the notion of absolute matter. Materiality is a manifestation of a special relation. Further, an element that is "material" with respect to one element may be a "pattern" with respect to some other.

Pattern as a Stable Change of Tissue

The terms "tissue" and "pattern" suggest questions about how a pattern is "painted" on the tissue. What is the nature of the "paint?" It is natural to regard the "paint" as some stable regularity characterizing the tissue. A pattern upon a pattern is a "regularity of a regularity."

We may suppose that the principal difference between living organisms endowed with minds and modern machines is that in the case of the former we have to do with long, perhaps closed chains of "tissue-pattern" relations, where each pattern represents a self-organizing system.[17] An ordinary machine is a chain consisting of a single relation tissue-pattern. "Physiology" can be viewed as a pattern on the field of atoms, "psychology" as a pattern drawn on physiology.

The model can be developed further in two directions. One could construct a hierarchy of systems, each connected to others by a tissue-pattern relation; or one can close the chain. In the latter case, the field of atoms turns out to be a pattern on the mind and at the same time a tissue on which the physiological events are patterns. Mind and body turn out to be intertwined in a single ontological scheme (cf., Figure 10.5).

In our opinion, the tissue-pattern relation is a useful methodological tool in investigating complex processes. At present, we are facing a chasm separating the phenomenology of mental processes from that of physical processes. It cannot be

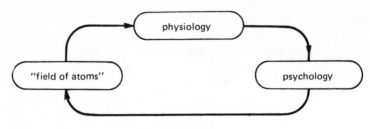

Figure 10.5

bridged by the old method. The tissue-pattern relation is juxtaposed in its logical construction to the traditional part-whole relation, which presently dominates an overwhelming majority of approaches to generalized systems.

The part whole relation was first completely formulated by Democritus, who introduced atoms as the absolute substantive elements from which bodies and events are assembled. The atoms were viewed as "responsible" for the properties of bodies, events being the bearers of qualitative attributes. In the tissue-pattern relation, the pattern is not a part of tissue. It is a phenomenon with its own laws of development. The connection between tissue and pattern is like that between the light bulbs and the text of a running advertisement. No matter how thoroughly we might investigate the electrical connections governing the movement of the letters on the advertisement, this will not help us to understand the text, its logical and linguistic structure, in a word, its meaning. Granted, the text cannot exist without the firld of light bulbs: An accident affecting the latter will destroy the text.

Attempts to resolve psycho-physiological dualism by reducing the psychological to the physiological are based on a faith in an irremovable "field of atoms," independent of macroobjects and serving to explain any manifestations of the latter. All attempts of this sort have failed, since they make the mind vanish. For this reason, we must seek new forms of representation and build new methods of reasoning.

Chapter 11

CONCLUDING REMARKS

Imagine a box that communicates with the investigator, a kind of object-partner. The investigator is interested in a number of questions such as whether the box understands him, to what extent and how the box can anticipate his thoughts, etc. How can the investigator get this information? The box can answer his questions. If the box cannot speak, the investigator can interpret its behavior, that is, undertake a reflexive description, endowing the box with motivations, goals, and an ability to carry out nontrivial reasoning. On the other hand, the investigator may have only a "physiological picture" of the box's body, however detailed and complete. Still, to interpret this picture, the investigator must undertake reflexive considerations and methods.

Suppose, for example, we wish to investigate the process of dreaming. We may describe the activity of the brain during dreams in arbitrary detail in structural-functional terms. But this description will not suffice for a dramatic description of the content of the dream. To describe this, we must employ

literary methods of representation, and these are instances of
reflexive methods. We can try to establish relations between
the physiological and the reflexive pictures. If we succeed,
we shall have a sort of configurator with two equally valid
projections of the process investigated.

Now imagine that the box is investigating the investigator.
The traditional juxtaposition of investigator and object loses
its validity. Both sides become both objects and investigators.
Both sides need reflexive representational means. Our reflexive analysis was undertaken to deal with situations of this
kind.

Psychologists have long been divided into naturalists and
artists. The former are equipped with structural and functional means; the latter with reflexive methods. The artists
were seldom interested in man's internal organs; the naturalists were seldom interested in relations among human beings.
The artist represents the object so as to put the viewer (or
reader) into a "semiotic space."

Imagine a painting depicting two people in conversation.
One expresses malicious gloating, the other suffering. The
viewer "hears" the conversation, but does not participate
in it. He is "plugged into" a model of semiotic environment
represented by the painting (cf., Figure 11.1). Communication "present" in the painting passes through the viewer.
We will call it *pseudocommunication*.[18] The viewer can see
reality through the eyes of the personae depicted. He can
imitate their thoughts about each other and even about himself if the images are looking at him!

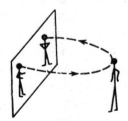

Figure 11.1

The technological revolution produced a new type of scientist equipped with engineering techniques. In studying complex systems, he has started to build specific information-processing simulations of such systems, unlike the physicist who had been concerned with the structural picture. The contemporary models that realize the functions of the scientific view of the world were created by physicists. They cannot include complex biological entities, let alone beings endowed with intellect.

In our opinion, a model, in order to serve as a picture of the world, must be a configurator with three projections: structural, evolving, and reflexive. The two-faced cosmology described in Chapter 9 illustrates the construction of a configurator. First, however, let us examine a variant of a model based on the two-faced cosmology that must arise in the mind of a physicist equipped with a "physical ideology."

Imagine a sheet pierced by rods (cf., Figure 11.2). The sheet can be folded to make a Moebius strip. The lengths of

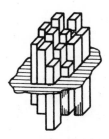

Figure 11.2

the rods will be chosen in such a way that if they are evened on one side, the lengths will be uniformly distributed on the other. This uniform distribution can be interpreted as a large degree of disorganization of a system, while a concentration of lengths in a small interval can be interpreted as a high degree of organization. In this way, not only the whole system but any part of it can be characterized by the distribution of lengths in that part. A living system will naturally appear as a highly organized region.

By folding the sheet into a Moebius strip, we assign a rule of proximity to the rods. Different cosmologies can be realized on that strip. We could try to realize literally the scheme described in Chapter 9. We can have the degree of organization tend toward a maximum while prescribing tendencies of highly organized systems, etc. In the process, configurations can probably be obtained that would be interesting to interpret from the point of view of physics or biology.

However, in terms of this cosmological construction, we cannot speak of the investigator as an element of the system. As we tried to demonstrate in Chapter 9, such theories can nevertheless show that the world is not confined within the framework of physical events. Yet these theories can say nothing about what exists beyond the framework.

Let us now undertake to construct a configurator. For simplicity, we shall use flat strips instead of rods. These strips can be moved independently. We line them up on one side of the dividing line to form a rectangle. On this rectangle we draw some smiling and some sad faces (Figure 11.3a). Next, we line up the strips below the dividing line and draw the same faces below. Clearly, by lining up the bottoms, we have distorted the faces above the line (cf., Figure 11.3b).

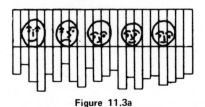

Figure 11.3a

Figure 11.3b

Now we can prescribe the game discussed in Chapter 9. Each face can become more or less distorted as it interacts with its "antipode" in accordance with the rules of the game. We have replaced the structural field of our rods (or strips) by a "holistic" structure of faces. Whereas the former physical model prescribed some theoretical cosmology as a system of structural units, we have introduced holistic units and have prescribed a mechanism to connect them to the standard units.

Now imagine an investigator who is presented with the functioning device represented in Figure 11.3b but who ignores the faces and attempts to describe the behavior of the system only in terms of the heights of the rods. Having created a sufficiently powerful mathematical apparatus, he will capture approximately the essential regularities of the system. Call the investigator a physicist.

Next, imagine an investigator who has not turned his attention to the strips. He has singled out the faces and is studying their evolution in time, the correlations between the distortions, etc. Call him a biologist.

Next, imagine a third investigator who is interested in the expressions of the faces and identifies with them, attempting to reconstruct their relations to each other and to reality and creates a typology of expressions. Call this investigator a psychologist.

Each investigator has his own subject matter, his own method of representation, and his own language.

Finally, imagine a fourth investigator in command of the integrated configuration. He is neither a physicist nor a biologist nor a psychologist. His model enables him to explain the problems presented to the physicist, the biologist, and the psychologist to the extent that he is familiar with their projections and constructions. Structural, evolving, and reflexive constructs are no longer separate, since the investigator sees the physical picture as the cause of the biological configurations and explains the mechanical motion of the strips by the adjusting actions of the faces. This picture has some features in common with those created by the artist. The faces smile and frown; that is a definition of a semiotic space present in the model. The investigator can plug himself into pseudocommunicative connections. This image of the world can include not only biological entities but also entities comparable to the investigator. In models of this sort, the investigator can finally deduce himself.

NOTES

1. The introduction of "+" is justified by operations to be defined below.

2. Here our method is essentially different from that of Heider (1946); Newcomb (1953); Laing, Phillipson, and Lee (1966); and Alperson (1975), where the main emphasis is on the investigation of contents reflected by the personae rather than on the reflexive structure in which these contents are immersed. A polynomial enables us to examine reflexive structures quite apart from other components of interactions between persons.

3. We note that the solution is perceived by X as his own if the element on which the solution depends is reflected by X in his inner world. Consider the form $(Ax + B)x$, where A and B are polynomials and where B is not representable as $B'x$. The solution of which A is the argument is perceived by X as his own: X "sees himself" making the decision. On the other hand, the solution of which B is the argument is not perceived by X as his own. The question arises whether such a solution is a solution in the traditional sense or whether we are dealing in the latter case with some "reaction."

4. Note that the operator of awareness $\omega = 1 + x + yx$, being "immersed" in a situation of this sort leads both players to disaster if they are both "equipped" with it; whereas in a purely antagonistic situation, as we have shown above, this operator generates a maximin solution. Thus the same operator can generate different types of behavior in different situations. We consider this fact to be most important, since it demonstrates the autonomy of reflexive processes with respect to behavior.

Translator's note: Actually, the "disaster" in the example cited is also a maximin solution as can be seen from the game matrix depicting this situation (cf., p. 65). It would be more accurate to say that the maximin principle leads to different sorts of outcome in different sorts of games. As an example, compare the following two games.

1, 1	−2, 1
2, −1	−1, −1

1, 1	−2, 1
2, −1	−10, −10

Prisoner's Dilemma   "Chicken"

In Prisoner's Dilemma, the maximin principle generates the outcome $(-1, 1)$, to which both players prefer $(1, 1)$. In "Chicken," the same principle generates $(1, 1)$, which both players prefer to $(-10, -10)$.

5. The "obviousness" of the choice reminds of "obviousness" in the thinking of the ancients, who attributed the fall of a stone to its heaviness.

6. In our algebra $oTxy \neq o$ (!). If we write a polynomial in the form $\Omega = T + (T + Tx + oTxy)x$, this means that the element Txy exists in X's inner world but it is "invisible" from X's position.

7. Of course, the verbal interpretation of the expression on the faces is mine. I am a particular "apparatus." Other "investigator-apparatuses" may not agree with me. But it must be admitted that a "true" verbal interpretation simply does not exist.

Chernoff (1973) employed the symbol of the cartoon face in a very interesting way, as a means for recording multivariate information with the help of that one symbol. There is an amusing relationship in the ways Chernoff and I use faces. He *expresses* "mathematical structures" with the help of affective symbols (faces), and I *insert* such symbols *into* "mathematical structures." Besides, Chernoff uses cartoon faces to represent multivariate information, and I use the cartoon faces to represent information which cannot be presented as a set of separate parameters. Initially, I included faces in special structures illustrating the processes of building models of the world which could not only reflect its physical and biological regularities but also include a reflection of the investigator and others like him (Lefebvre, 1967). Such a use of faces, however, was allegorical rather than constructional in character. It assumed its constructional nature only when I applied the symbol of cartoon faces to introreflexive polynomials (Lefebvre, 1973a; 1973b; 1975).

The need for the visual presentation of information is particularly acute nowadays (Zinchenko, 1971). The recipient of mathematical or verbal information has to submit it to additional analysis. Frequently this analysis is so difficult as to negate the value of the available information. The problems of presenting information visually are discussed by Huggins and Entwisle (1974), who have also compiled a detailed annotated bibliography on this subject.

8. Pairs of opposite nodes are designated in Table 3 (cf., p. 129).

9. Note that the relation "opposite" permits the traveler to remain on the second level in consequence of certain instructions. For this reason, the traveler did not pass to the first level on the seventh and eight moves. On the tenth move, the traveler "disobeys," but since he is on the first level, he must leave it. The "disobedience" is registered by the noncoincidence of solid and dotted arrows.

10. The reader may want to consult the scheme shown in Figure 5.5.

11. This is valid if the probability of reaching the gate from each of the nodes preceding the gate is 0.5. This assumption is justified by the linear structure of the maze.

12. Here we have resorted to an artifice, supposing that the situation determines the number of perceptions, while the number of perceptions determines the coefficient.

13. Similar models could be based on the idea of signal-flow graphics (S. J. Mason, 1952; W. H. Huggins and D. R. Entwisle, 1968).

A very interesting approach, which connects the reflexive polynomials with ethical problems of decision-making in special games, was founded by A. F. Trudoliubov (1972) and developed by A. L. Toom (1973, 1974).

14. The author is grateful to G. P. Schchedrovitsky for a fruitful discussion of this model.

15. The author is grateful to G. E. Zhuraviev, I. M. Krein, and G. L. Smolian for interesting discussions of this question.

16. A methodological investigation can be expressed in a similar manner. If the methodologist is designated by x_4, the situation will appear as

$$(\Omega_1 + \Omega_2 + \Omega_3 + \Omega_4)x_4.$$

The methodologist himself recognizes the mechanism that reduces one systemic conception to another.

17. Note that in constructing the two-faced cosmology in the previous chapter, we have already essentially utilized the "tissue-pattern" relation. We put two patterns on the opposite sides of one "sheet." After having turned the sheet into a Moebius strip, we created a single pattern "juxtaposed to itself."

18. This sort of communication must be distinguished from the communication between the artist and the viewer, manifested in the painting. Actually, the latter consists of transmitting a certain "semiotic space" containing pseudo-communications.

REFERENCES

ALPERSON, B., "In Search of Buber's Ghosts: A Calculus for Interpersonal Phenomenology," *Behavioral Science,* Vol. 20, 1975.

ASHBY, W. R., "Principles of Self-Organization," H. Von Foerster and G. W. Zopf, Jr., eds., *Principles of Self-Organization.* Oxford, Eng.: Pergamon, 1962.

BARANOV, P. V. and A. F. TRUDOLIUBOV, "Ob odnoi igre cheloveka s avtomatom, provodiashchim refleksivnoe upravlenie" (On a game between a human subject and an automaton exercising reflexive control.), *Problemy Evristiki,* Moscow: Vysshaia Shkola, 1969a.

− − − , "O vosmozhnosti sozdania shemy refleksivnogo upravienia nezavisimoi ot siuzheta eksperimentalno-igrovoi situatsii" (On the possibility of constructing a scheme of reflexive control independent of the game-experimental situation), *Problemy Evristiki,* Moscow: Vysshaia Shkola, 1969b.

BLAUBERG, I. V., V. N. SADOVSKI, and E. G. YUDIN, *Sistemnyi podhod: predposylki, problemy, trudnosti* (The systems approach: Assumptions, problems, and difficulties.). Moscow: Znanie, 1969.

BOHR, N., *The Unity of Knowledge,* New York: Doubleday, 1955.

BONGARD, M., *Pattern Recognition,* East Lansing, Mich.: Spartan, 1970.

CHATTERJEE, S. and D. DATTA, *An Introduction to Indian Philosophy.* Calcutta: University of Calcutta, 1954.

CHERNOFF, G., "The Use of Faces to Represent Points of k-dimensional Space Graphically," *Journal of the American Statistical Association* 68, 342, pp. 361-368, 1973.

EDDINGTON, A. S., *The Mathematical Theory of Relativity,* Cambridge: at the University Press, 1924.

GALPERIN, P. Ya., "Psihologia myshlenia i uchenie o poetapnom formirovanii umstvennyh deistvii" (The psychology of thought and a theory of sequential formation of mental acts.) *Issledovanie myshlenia v sovetskoi psihologii,* Moscow: Nauka, 1966.

HEIDER, F., "Attitudes and Cognitive Organization," *Journal of Psychology,* Vol. 21, 1946.

HUGGINS, W. H. and D. R. ENTWISLE, *Iconic Communication: An Annotated Bibliography*, Baltimore and London: Johns Hopkins, 1974.
———, *Introductory Systems and Design*, Waltern, Mass.: Blaisdell, 1968.

LAING, R. D., H. PHILLIPSON, and A. R. LEE, *Interpersonal Perception*, New York: Springer, 1966.
LEFEBVRE, V. A., "O sposobah predstavlenia obektov kak sistem" (On methods of representing objects as systems), *Logika Nauchnogo Issledovania* (Theses of Reports), Kiev: Kiev State University, 1962.
———, "Ishodnye idei logiki refleksivnyh igr" (Basic ideas of the logic of reflexive games), *Problemy Issledovania Sistem i Struktur*, Moscow: Academy of Sciences of the USSR Press, 1965a.
———, "O samoorganizuiushchihsa i samorefleksivnyh sistemah i ih issledovanii" (On self-organizing and self-reflexive systems), *Problems Issledovania Sistem i Struktur*, Moscow: Academy of Sciences of the USSR Press, 1965b.
———, "Elementy logiki refleksivnyh igr" (Elements of logic of reflexive games), *Problemy ingenernoi psihologii*, No. 4, 1966.
———, *Konfliktuiushchie struktury* (Conflicting structures), Moscow: Vysshaia Shkola, 1967.
———, BARANOV, P. V., and V. E. LEPSKY, "Vnutrennyaya valyuta v refleksivnyh igrah" (Internal currency in reflexive games), *Tehnicheskaya kibernetika, Academy of Sciences of the USSR News*, No. 4, 1969.
LEFEBVRE, V. A., "Sistemy, sravnimye s issledovatelem po sovershenstvu" (Systems comparable to the investigator in their degree of perfection), *Sistemnye issledovania*, Moscow: Nauka, 1969a.
———, "Ustroistva, optimiziruyushchie svoyu rabotu v rezultate protivodeistvia cheloveka" (Devices that optimize their performance as a consequence of interference by man), *Problemy Evristiki*, Moscow: Vysshaia Shkola, 1969b.
———, "Janus-Kosmologie," *Ideen des exakten Wissens*, No. 6, 1969c.
———, "Das System im System," *Ideen des exakten Wissens*, No. 10, 1970.
———, "Formalnyi metod issledovania refleksivnyh protsessov" (A formal method of studying reflexive processes), *Voprosy Filosofii*, No. 9, 1971.
———, "A Formal Method of Investigating Reflective Processes," *General Systems*, Vol. XVII, pp. 181-188, 1972.
———, *Konfliktuiushchie struktury* (Conflicting structures, new enlarged ed.), Moscow: Sovetskoe Radio Press, 1973a.
———, "Auf dem Wege zur psychographischen Mathematik," *Ideen des exakten Wissens*, No. 6, 1973b.
———, "Iconic Calculus: Symbols With Feeling in Mathematical Structures," *General Systems*, Vol. XX, 1975.
———, "Introreflective Analysis," *Behavioral Science*, Vol. 22, No. 1, 1977.
LEONTIEV, A. N., *Problemy razvitia psihiki* (Problems of psychic development), Moscow: Mysl, 1965.
LIDELL-HART, B. H., *The Strategy of Indirect Approach*, London: Faber & Faber, 1941, p. 305.
LINEBARGER, P.M.A., *Psychological Warfare*, Washington, D.C.: Combat Forces Press, 1954.

LOFGREN, L., "Automata of High Complexity Methods of Increasing Their Reliability by Redundancy," *Information and Control,* 1, 127, 1958.

MASON, S. F., "Feedback Theory–Some Properties of Signal Flow Graphs," *Proceedings of the I.R.E.,* September, 1952.

MOORE, E. F., "Mathematics in The Biological Science," *Scientific American,* 9, 1964.

Von NEUMANN, J., *Theory of Selfreproducing Automata,* Urbana, Ill.: Univ. of Illinois Press, 1966.

NEWCOMB, T. M., "An Approach to the Study of Communicative Acts," *Psychological Review,* 6, 1953.

RAPOPORT, A., "Some Game Theoretical Aspects of Parasitism and Symbiosis," *Bulletin of Mathematical Biophysics,* Vol. 18, 1956.

––– , "The Experimental Investigation of Parameters of Self-Organization in Groups of Three Subjects," H. Von Foerster and G. W. Zopf, Jr., eds., *Principles of Self-Organization,* Oxford, Eng.: Pergamon, 1962.

––– , *Strategy and Conscience,* New York: Harper & Row, 1964.

––– and A. M. CHAMAH, *Prisoner's Dilemma,* Ann Arbor: Univ. of Michigan Press, 1965.

SCHEDROVITSKY, G. P., "Zametki o myshlenii po shemam dvoinogo znania" (Notes on thinking according to schemes of two-valued knowledge), *Materialy k simpoziumu po logike nauki,* Kiev: Naukova dumka, 1966.

––– , "Configuration as a Method of Structuring Complex Knowledge," *Systematics,* Vol. 8, No. 4, 1971.

SCHELLING, T., *The Strategy of Conflict,* Cambridge, Mass.: Harvard University Press, 1960.

TOOM, A. L., "Sposoby priniatia reshenii v odnom klasse igr" (The means of decision-making in a special class of games), *Isvestia Akademii Nauk USSR, Technicheskaja Kibernetika,* No. 3, 1973.

––– and A. F. TRUDOLIUBOV, "Reflexive Wechselbeziehungen im Kollektiv," *Ideen des exakten Wissens,* No. 3, 1974.

TRUDOLIUBOV, A. F., "Reshenie na setiah zavisimostei i reflexivnye mnogochleny" (Decisions on graphs and reflexive polynomials), *VI Symposium in Cybernetics,* Tbilisi, 1972.

TSETLIN, M. L., "Automaton Theory and Modeling of Biological Systems," *Mathematics in Science and Engineering,* Vol. 102, New York and London: Academic Press, 1973.

VYGOTSKY, L. S., *Myshlenie i rech* (Thought and speech), Moscow: OGIZ-SOTSEKGIZ, 1934.

ZINCHENKO, V. P., "Productive Perception," *Voprosy psihologii,* No. 6, 1971.

ABOUT THE AUTHOR

VLADIMIR A. LEFEBVRE is currently a lecturer in Russian literature, Program in Russian, University of California at Irvine. He was born in Leningrad and received the equivalents of a Ph.D. in psychology and of an M.A. in mathematics from Lomonosov Moscow State University. In 1974 he emigrated from the Soviet Union to the United States. Dr. Lefebvre is the author of about forty publications dealing with his main fields of interest, cognitive processes, human reflexion, hierarchical relationships in small groups, literature and psychology, and philosophical problems in psychology. His publications have appeared in several languages including English, German, and Japanese.